TRAJECTORY

ELEVATE your selling skills now!
Transform from salesperson to
SALES PROFESSIONAL

Stella
Happy Birthday!
Enjoy —

Feb 3/22.

GREG BALKWILL CSP

ISBN: 978-1-7773860-0-9 (Paperback)
ISBN: 978-1-7773860-1-6 (eBook)

DEDICATION

Nobody succeeds in life walking the journey alone. I have had many people walk with me providing a great deal of support, but one has walked beside me for 39 years. My wife Elli has seen most of my entire career in the arena I call professional sales. She has endured the valley experiences that have come with life in general, and has shown a great deal of resilience and courage while believing in me and celebrating my successes. She has laughed at my jokes and endured my humor for almost 40 years. I love her dearly. We have created a great partnership with our most celebrated reward being our two daughters, Katelyn and Janelle. They too, have had a front row seat to my journey, providing an enormous degree of encouragement while ensuring I laughed often. I am so proud of 'who they are'. The first draft editing was completed with my family, so thank you all for the hours invested making my goal of writing this book come true.

So to Elli, Katelyn and Janelle—you are my three stars. Thanks for shining your light into my life. Love from me.

THANKS FOR READING TRAJECTORY. As a personal and sincere thanks I want to provide you a free gift just for reading it. Go to **www.gregbalkwill.com** to receive your gift. My suggestion is to print, laminate and carry this resource with you from this day forward. Thanks again. Good Selling!

CONTENTS

INTRODUCTION

In 1992 John Michael Montgomery wrote a country song with these lyrics:

"Life's a dance, You learn as you go
Sometimes you lead, sometimes you follow
Don't worry about what you don't know
Life's a dance, you learn as you go"

I recall, with headphones on, belting out this song, as I walked the beach on Treasure Island, Florida. I now realize that while this continues to be one of my all time favourite songs, it also mirrors my journey in professional selling. I learned as I went along. I didn't worry about what I didn't know but through that, I made a lot of costly selling mistakes.

Whether you are female or male you must be considering or have begun your career in professional selling. It matters not what you are selling today. This book is for you. You don't have to wander around for a decade wondering what to do next. You will learn instant practical steps to the selling process. My four decades of success in professional selling will guide you around the landmines and deep potholes that I firmly stepped (or sometimes rapidly fell) into, ensuring you don't make the same mistakes

I did. You will read many funny stories about real life sales calls where I both succeeded and failed. I'll tell you straight up what to do and what NOT to do in effort to see you succeed immediately in your selling career. Consider this your road map to selling success!

Additionally, you will discover that once your skills are well developed you can sell anything!

Looking back, my sales journey began as a 9 year old boy in Essex, Ontario. I began going door to door seeking customers who wanted their lawn cut. I soon had a small business. Unbeknownst to me, I had just completed my first sale. I sold many products as a pre-teen and teenager, including poinsettias for a Minor Hockey fundraiser and 400 boxes of Christmas cards (during a postal strike) at our church youth group. I started a rabbit business selling to market, had an animal feeds distributorship, trained and sold Quarter Horses, raised and sold registered Australian Shepherd dogs, and sold a tire balancing sealant product. My first full-time selling role was at a Life Insurance company at 22, then at 24 I moved to the electrical distributor construction sector. Later in my selling journey, for 10 years I sold fluid power products (pneumatic and hydraulic). In addition to my 'real jobs', my wife and I have spent nearly 40 years purchasing, renovating, and flipped many houses. We've often been landlords as well! Regardless of the feat at hand, sales skills and people skills were required.

I have experienced a lot of satisfying success in professional sales, winning many awards, plaques, trophies, and of course, was rewarded financially as well. Some of the highest income earners in the world have created wealth via their professional sales careers.

This book will teach you the *selling process*. You will be taught the *6-pack of selling*, and learn *how to create the success triangle*, a skill absolutely necessary to succeed in selling professionally. Additionally, I will outline why *goal setting* is so critical to your journey. I address the topic of *self talk* and how to respond to those interior voices you'll hear. I will teach you how to present and conduct yourself in a professional fashion. I have coached and mentored many, and seen them grow from where you are now, to Sales Professionals.

I am very excited to have you read the interviews I call the ***Voice of Experience*** where I share candid stripped down interviews with 6 successful sellers. These voices come from people in all stages of their careers, selling their product of choice.

Sprinkled throughout the book are what I call **BALKTALKS**. These gold nuggets offer tidbits of critical advice. In addition to these talks, I included the ***code of ethics*** clearly defined by the Canadian Professional Sales Association.

If you want your professional trajectory to lead to improvement and success, read on. If you have a passion for selling and are prepared to learn and apply the methodologies I provide, this is exactly the book you need. Don't hesitate. I promise that this play book will assist you in maneuvering around the detours and barriers, and direct you toward selling success. Why bother with trial and error? Your employer will want an immediate return on their investment, and after reading this book you will be well equipped to provide that.

Ordinary people can accomplish extraordinary success with the right tools. Are you ready to rise to the top?

1

MY JOURNEY TOWARD PROFESSIONAL SELLING

IF YOU'VE GOTTEN this far, you are obviously considering a career as a Sales Professional or are in the early phase of your journey. Perhaps this book was gifted to you as a roadmap to your selling success, or you found it online or at your favorite bookstore. Regardless, congratulations on entering the arena. You are in for an exciting and exhilarating journey, and I wish you much success.

I recently found myself wondering where my passion for sales originated and how it developed. As mentioned in the introduction, I was nine years old when my dad purchased a new Toro self-propelled gas mower and it seemed like an ideal time to start a lawn care business. I quickly had three lawns to cut. Two were for widowed ladies nearby who would also have me run their grocery errands on my bike. *This represents my first door to door selling*—asking for the opportunity to provide a service in exchange for money. I was in heaven. A couple years later we moved to a farm and started raising Quarter Horses. I'll come back to that later, but when that move occurred, my lawn care and errand running business ended.

The next phase of my sales journey occurred at 13 years old. I vividly recall my first horse show. I was a nervous wreck. There was an event called Showmanship at Halter where all youth 18 and younger 'showed' their horse to a judge. While leading the horse, the judging was based on one's ability to walk and trot to and away from a judge in a very straight line ensuring that the grooming of the animal and myself was impeccable. In my first show I took home a second place ribbon in Showmanship. Between this first show and the remainder of my Youth Showmanship career to 18 years old I won 100% of the classes entered in that category. We showed horses every weekend from May to October each year, and dozens of first place ribbons and trophies were won in that one event. Riding events also occurred at each show and again were judged on riding skills and showmanship in saddle, known as Junior Equitation. I didn't win each week but won dozens of trophies over the many years of horse showing. Between my dad and I, we won over 200 trophies. All but 3 trophies were donated back to the Junior Horsemen's Association many years later. Looking back, I can clearly see how showing horses truly assisted me in my professional sales career in seeing the *critical importance of developing effective planning, preparation and presentation skills.* If a kid had a great horse but didn't present it well, he or she would not win. The judging was not based on horse pedigree but on my ability to showcase my product. Showing horses taught *me how to win humbly, lose graciously and be happy for those who did win.*

At 14 years old I started a rabbit business. I purchased a large white Flemish Giant buck and a few does (females), and began breeding, raising, and selling 4 pound rabbits to market. Eventually I had around 60 rabbits regularly producing bunnies every 28 days or so. I negotiated an agreement with a woman who had her own contract with a grocery chain who bought rabbits, and we cut a deal. I was making money. This rabbit business was very profitable until one winter evening. My rabbits were in a small outbuilding about 20x8ft filled with tiers of cages. The wooden building had a latch on the door but not a lock. Upon walking to feed my rabbits the door was open and the latch ripped off. An animal had gotten into the rabbitry and killed all but one of my rabbits. I suspect many died of fright but some were obviously attacked. I never discovered what killed them but it must have been a dog or coyote. At any rate I still had one rabbit—my Flemish Giant buck. One day a friend asked to borrow my buck to breed some does over the weekend; considering I had no does to breed, I loaned him out. On Monday he called and said my buck died over the weekend. Upon probing he admitted to putting my buck in a large pen with several does. Either they killed him or he died a happy death. I was now out of the rabbit business. Regardless, ***my entrepreneurial drive was developing***. I had some sales skills, some communication skills, a few negotiating skills, and was not nearly as fearful approaching adults as I once was. Again, the rearview mirror shows all these experiences contributed to my eventual selling journey.

My next business transaction was at 16: and I finally had a driver's license. During my childhood and adolescence, I played plenty of minor hockey. Many local hockey associations required a Christmas tournament fundraiser. Luckily, my dad knew a man who owned a large flower growing greenhouse operation in Ruthven, Ontario. My entrepreneurial skills took over again: I bought several thousand poinsettias and resold them to the Minor Hockey Associations in my area. Each transaction doubled the price point. Eventually, poinsettias sold for $10.00 each. Even though my family always supported my businesses, I really had to hustle to sell all of them in time for Christmas—my Mom only bought two. I could sense something brewing in my gut regarding sales but it would be a few more years before it all made sense.

Summer months were always full of farming and raising horses. At 17 I had been training and showing horses for a few years already. Between the ages of 14 and 17, I began to raise and sell foals. Selling horses was yet another chapter in my journey. With help from my Dad, I learned to assess horse value, ensuring bloodlines and show performance all aligned with a selling price.

Over the next number of years *I learned to negotiate* the buying and selling of horses and tack. I invested some of my time training and showing other people's horses for the purpose of getting points and raising values. As a young man, this ***taught me how to converse with adults,*** seek win/win negotiations, and earned me some money in the horse business. My most satisfying transaction was buying a one-day-old foal for $3,000. As a yearling she won 7th of 104 entries at the largest National Quarter Horse show (Quarterama) in Canada, and I sold her for $8,000 shortly thereafter.

Working on a horse ranch demanded a work ethic that likely would not have developed had we not moved to a farm. Raising animals required that they be fed at regular intervals each morning and evening and that their stalls and surroundings be kept clean and safe. Grooming and training was done daily during show season. The tack was polished before every show, and then came hay and straw season when we baled enough to last a year. The temperature in that hay loft as we got closer and closer to the metal roof was a killer, but as I say, ***the work ethic was developing quickly.*** In my spare time I had an acre of grass to cut each week, fences to mend or paint and that was on top of everyday chores! There wasn't much leisure time, and ***managing my time*** became a skill learned early in life through the myriad of tasks required, while juggling a personal life as well.

I learned a plethora of lessons in the horse business. It clearly provided a massive stepping stone to heading toward a career in professional selling.

I didn't know it then but my sales career had actually begun.

By 17, I discovered I had some transferable skills. Selling flowers, horses, rabbits, or dogs required similar selling skills or sales strategies. I was really enjoying the people side of the business too. I was learning how to transact, and seeing a bit of success was very motivating. Because I was still in high school, having extra pocket money was a bonus. As soon as I graduated I bought a brand new Monte Carlo.

Following high school, where I studied electricity for four years, I began an apprenticeship with a local contractor. I didn't make a firm commitment to becoming an electrician at this point, though, and I eventually moved on to work at a large utility company where my dad worked. It was very enticing: the pay was double! Shortly after joining the utility company, there came an opening to bid on a new position in another department. The advantage was that when the task was completed each day, the employee could go home, yet be paid for eight hours. I would hustle to finish by noon and then get back to the farm to complete my other duties.

The angst in my gut for selling was still there and at 20, and with a job that allowed me to leave when my task was completed, I started my own animal feeds distributorship. I was now marketing, selling, and then delivering horse, dog, and rabbit feed. In order to make this role happen, I needed to purchase a large truck to transport all the products. Yet again, this job meant cold calling. I began calling on ranches, kennels, and rabbitries. I aimed to convince them that my feed was superior to what they were currently feeding their animals. The business grew, but the 100-pound bags of grain grew heavier each week. While my sales skills seemed to improve, my business knowledge lacked. I didn't know what to do with this growing business. I didn't earn enough profit to hire help, and the physical workload killed my back—it had been hurt when a horse fell on me inside a horse trailer a couple years prior.

One day, I presented my dog food to a prominent breeder. She invited me into her house. She had no furniture other than a kitchen table and two chairs. Instead, the entire house was filled with dog pens and dozens of dogs, some chained to heat registers. All the dogs barked like crazy. As I presented the features and health benefits of my brand, the breeder asked if I had ever tasted my dog food myself. I recall looking at her awaiting a laugh, when she reached into a bowl of her dog food and woofed down a handful. I conceded defeat and left. There was no sale happening here that day, or ever.

I eventually sold all my stock and the truck and decided to re-route my selling skills. I knew I really enjoyed the thrill of selling stuff. I just needed to find out what that stuff would be. Over the next year, I sold purple goop called Commercial Balancing Sealant with the claim that when injected into huge transport or farm tires, it would automatically balance the tires and save the owner thousands of dollars in tire balancing costs. Since the tires would always be in balance, they'd wear evenly and last longer. It was a tough sell. The guys driving transport trucks really scared me. Intimidation was something new, as I had never experienced fear while making a sales call. I had some scattered success once again, but no real passion for the product.

Time to find a real sales job.

2

BUILD YOUR SELLING SKILL SET

THE JOURNEY I took toward becoming a Sales Professional has taken many twists and turns, including some part time selling roles, two of which were in men's clothing stores. A man in a nearby small town of Harrow, Ontario, owned a high quality menswear store and offered me a weekend job. He was a key mentor in my journey, even if he never knew it. I watched this man closely as he greeted customers in his store. I saw how he asked the right questions and presented different suits, ties, shirts, and belts, provided options and asked about budgets. He was a true gentleman and provided a high level of respect to each customer. I copied what I saw, and one day many years later he offered me the opportunity to purchase his business. My wife and I had just moved to another city and had a young family, so the timing didn't fit—but this was a glance into the kinds of successes I *could* have.

I had an acquaintance in the life insurance industry who convinced me to get my license. I already had a full-time job at the utility company, but they refused to allow me to join their sales department. The company said

I was too young to be successful at sales; I was 22 but admittedly looked younger. So, I agreed to get my license, and began selling life insurance in my spare afternoons and evenings. After a year of part-time selling, I was making more money part-time than I was full-time at the utility company. I had just finished reading a book by Robert Schuller called *Move Ahead With Possibility Thinking*. It was a life changer. I resigned my job at the utility and began selling life insurance full-time.

Our office practiced mock sales calls by the hour, which really improved my presentation skills. My closing percentage was spectacular. I was winning awards regularly and was in the top 50 sellers globally in our company for two years running. Because my key client targets, those close to my own age, could only be seen in the evenings, my daytime hours became somewhat unproductive. I discovered that some younger clients would cancel their policy when any monetary challenges came up in their lives. At the same time, I started listening to the voices in my own head that told me that people hated insurance salesmen. I would sense or imagine people avoiding me in certain social settings. This had a dramatically negative impact on my motivation, **(I talk about 'voices' in chapter 12.)** and shortly thereafter I chose to leave the industry. I thoroughly enjoyed the income, but not the working hours. I had to be honest with myself and assess that this selling chapter of my life provided great experience, but that my passion for selling life insurance was not the fit that I had imagined.

Around this time I saw an ad where an electrical wholesale distributor was seeking a new employee. As an apprentice I had visited the location many times to pick up goods. I knew they had sales people, but this role was for a warehouse worker. I thought "Hey—I have 4 years of high school electrical theory, a couple years of practical electrical work experience and some sales experience so maybe I can start at the advertised role and work my way into a selling role." I applied and was hired. I began as a shipper-receiver. Within 8 months, I was promoted to counter sales, and quickly to inside sales, where I honed my phone selling skills. Within another year I was offered a promotion to a branch in another city as a counter supervisor, overseeing staff and inventory processes in the warehouse and counter sales areas. My sales juices were really flowing, and I realized my next step would be a full-time outside sales role.

Before it happened, though, I knew I needed even more sales experience. In this new city, I started a part-time sales role at Elk's Menswear. I worked each day at my full-time job and for three years worked at the menswear store nights and weekends. I loved the job, and being on commission was highly motivating. Because I had an awesome discount on clothing purchases, I was also pretty well dressed!

Then the selling door opened at the electrical distributorship. I was offered the opportunity to leave the branch one day per week and see if I could develop any new business. I was only permitted to call on customers who were not buying from our company at that time. Each Tuesday I would leave the branch and head to areas where I knew few other competitors were going. One particular customer lived an hour from my home base, in a small village called Arkona. I was gaining a lot of selling confidence from the clothing business and previous sales roles. My first sale was $96.30 from the Arkona contractor but within a few years, my sales to him grew to over $200,000 annually. After one year of part-time selling I was awarded a full-time sales job with a brand new company car, expense card for fuel, paid insurance, and commissions too! I finally felt like I had found my niche—a full-time sales role, selling a tangible product to people who actually wanted and needed what I was selling. It was perfect.

Note that I was willing to put in extensive time and effort to build my selling skill set. I realized I would not work in a men's clothing store as my full-time career, but I used the three year opportunity to polish the skills I had developed from previous selling roles. *I created an effective series of open-ended questions for clients, learned to be comfortable with appropriate eye contact, sharpened my closing skills, improved my overall customer service, and learned how to fold shirts and sweaters at the end of each shift. If you are new to selling, get all the experience you can, selling anything you can.* The retail sector provides great opportunities for experience, but as you have read, my journey saw me sell many products through several business sectors. Each contributed greatly to my success. Don't necessarily focus on or commit to one sector for now. Get experience first and find your perfect fit later. All you learn will be transferred to your next role. If you have already selected your career path, congratulations. You are on your way to a successful career in professional selling.

For you newer Sales Professionals, it is good for you to know just how rewarding your career can become once you see quality relationships and friendships building. The man who bought that first order of $96.30 eventually became a good friend. There came an opportunity to introduce him to a general contractor I knew who was a commercial builder. That customer was then provided the opportunity to perform the electrical work on a new Nursing Home for the general contractor. This dramatically impacted my friend's business. Even then, it was critical to develop a network—in this case, it was mutually beneficial. One evening, this customer and his wife took my wife and I out for supper and thanked me for the part I played in strengthening and growing his business. In return, my new friend Henk Goertz, introduced me to his brother who was in manufacturing and began to buy a lot of products from me. This story is one of many successes where the network and relationships I've built impacted my selling success; this story was the highlight of my career at that time.

My wife and family spent 10 years in Sarnia, Ontario, and my sales career flourished. I was fortunate to have a good manager with excellent sales skills and great support from the inside sales team. Sales Professionals cannot succeed without strong support. Much of my success in my 35 years in industrial sales can be traced back to team support. Throughout my years in the electrical outside sales role, I achieved top 3 sales awards year after year provincially, and earned second once. Three of the top sellers (including me!) were promoted to branch managers and so my next journey began.

I was now 37 and a branch manager. For the next decade or so, I was responsible for the profitability of my branch operation. I quickly learned that what my previous manager had said was accurate: he told me that I would have no problem with the revenue side of the business, but that people will drive me nuts. I laughed when he said that since he made it look easy. He was excellent at both sides of the business but had a different temperament than me. We worked well together most of the time. I dive into the importance of assessing temperaments later, as it is a critical aspect to succeeding in professional selling. Our profit centre saw substantial growth over those years, and it was once awarded Branch of the Year. I was also awarded Branch Manager of the Year across the province once. This again, was a total team success.

Over a period of a number of years, I had been pursued by one of our largest customers. He had purchased a small electrical contracting company, with a goal of extreme expansion and had invited me to become his GM. The goal was to expand to a total services group. After 22 years I resigned my post as branch manager, and joined his team. The company grew to 56 staff and a fleet of 18 trucks. There were 4 unionized groups under one roof, servicing the auto and steel industrial sectors. This man was the most generous boss I had ever seen or experienced. He treated his staff like royalty, often buying large gifts of appreciation, and giving raises when not necessary. He always went beyond the call of duty to ensure his staff was happy and content. We all worked extra hard to reciprocate our appreciation. I worked for him for 4 years, but since I was in a managerial / administrative role, I was not scratching my itch—selling!

After I resigned from that role, I had a period of 6 months of unemployment while I was searching for the right sales fit. One day, a friend attended his grandma's funeral, and his wife's cousin was there from Toronto. His pneumatic and hydraulic technologies company was finding it challenging to find a salesperson to service the Windsor area. His past hires had not worked out, as they had required heavy monitoring and didn't actually do the work to succeed. My friend suggested that I should be pursued, and I received a call from Toronto. After hearing the sales pitch on why I should join the company, and admitting I had no knowledge of fluid power technology, I stated with sincere thanks that "While your company sounds awesome, I can honestly say I have nothing to offer your company." I thanked him and we hung up. About 6 weeks later he called again and we repeated the conversation, but this time I agreed to join him for lunch.

I joined this organization as a technical sales representative, covering a fairly large Ontario corridor from Windsor to London. I knew absolutely nothing about fluid power, but attended heavy training sessions for weeks on end in Mississauga, Ontario. Over the next 10 years I saw that training was a key attribute to the company's success. The business was employee owned, which was a substantial key to employee retention and profitability focus. In my first year at this corporation I was fortunate enough to be awarded the National Chairman's Sales Award for sales and profit growth. This was the top sales award in Canada. The fact is, the outstanding team behind me contributed substantially to the award. I had brought some transferable skills to the table and admittedly some selling process expertise, while the inside staff and other extremely knowledgeable sales pros and suppliers provided the technical expertise. Upper management recognized that while most of the sales staff were extremely competent technically, they needed someone to teach the sales process, and so I was asked to become a district sales manager, a shared role with another man. We split Ontario and Manitoba. Aurelio Romano was a technical genius and had a great likability factor with refined sales skills. I learned more from him than he likely learned from me, but we enjoyed sharing the role. A year later, it was decided the sales team should have one voice directing them and I was asked to become the regional sales manager, working alongside all the technical sales reps in both provinces. This role required weekly travel and hotel stays about 100 nights a year. I ate a lot of meals alone. I enjoyed this 10 year chapter of my life but it ended with me being fired, shortly after the naming of a new president. The company had decided to take the sales team in a different direction.

Following my firing, my wife and I decided to move to Western Canada where both our daughters had moved. I spent the next year pondering the next chapter of my life, but one day through my LinkedIn profile I received a call from a headhunter asking if I would take on a trailblazer selling role for another electrical distributor. The role required sales coverage of a very large territory, working with two key branch operations. I accepted that role and again, I was back in my selling glory. However, selling became more challenging because I was living in a province where I only knew one person—my daughter. Regardless, I accepted the challenge, and with two strong teams of inside support we did very well. In my first year there I was presented an award for having the largest growth in stock sales for the Western Region. Enough growth had occurred within the territory that when I retired four years later, they replaced me with two sales people. Interestingly enough, when I was hired, the challenge presented to me was exactly that—when you retire ensure the territory can support 2. Many superb internal customers contributed to the success of that challenge. Then I retired and wrote this book.

BALKTALK #1 – You are Always on Stage.

You will recall that I watched the owner of the men's clothing store closely and aligned my actions with his. He didn't necessarily see me observing him but he was most definitely on stage. As a Sales Professional you will be observed each day of your selling career. Those observing you will be customers, teammates, suppliers, competitors, friends, relatives, family, and anyone you meet. We all are assessed within 7 seconds of being met so it is imperative that your appearance is always professional and your behaviour friendly. If you are a parent, you already know how our kids emulate what they see and say, from us. This kind of mimicking occurs in the workplace as well. If you desire a positive business culture, be the one who brings that positive energy to the workplace. As a young inside sales person, I watched a particular outside salesman each day. He always had a smile on his face, and his favorite line was "Never complain, never explain." Negativity can become a trap if your cultural surroundings are toxic or overly negative, but we all have the option to either participate or contribute to a more positive team environment. Rest assured—somebody is watching you. Be the best version of yourself possible. You are on stage!

3

"GET RIPPED"—DEVELOP THE 6 PACK OF SELLING

IN THIS CHAPTER, I unpack a group of skillsets or selling disciplines required to 'get ripped.' While I admit to not having six pack abs, I can say with confidence my selling skills have become 'ripped' over these decades. Time to hit the gym.

1) Planning & Preparation

Zig Ziglar states "You don't have to be great to start, but you have to start to be great." Let's get started.

If you've been in sales for a week and have a sales manager, coach, or mentor you have likely heard that *failing to plan is planning to fail.* Nobody wants or plans to fail, yet actions taken toward selling success must be well planned.

Planning is a melting pot of every strategy you develop prior to taking action. You must set time aside to plan and prepare. This in, and of itself is a discipline, since it can take on a life of its own. I have coached certain people who love the planning process but at times have observed it turning into what is called the 'paralysis of analysis.' At some point you need to get out of the dugout, grab a bat, and start swinging for the fences.

Two specific areas of planning for a sales-based position include planning your day's regular activities and planning your actual sales calls for the day. There are a myriad of actions and requirements that can impact actual selling time. Multitasking and effective time management is a must. What we'd all like to do is sell and make money. If you're not careful, the entire day will be consumed with planning, without the productivity required to exceed your sales budget and get paid.

From the moment your alarm rings, so much can get jammed into the day: showering, breakfast, reviewing yesterday's sales, funnel management, checking month-to-date results, CRM software data input, reviewing the day's activities and selling calls, travelling between appointments, traffic jams, follow up on the commitments you made yesterday to customers and clients, touching base with the office, delegating activities that allow you to be more productive today, following up on yesterday's quotes or presentations, replying to emails that came in late yesterday if you haven't done so, returning any phone calls that came in while you were selling yesterday, eating lunch with a customer, emergency problems and solutions, company-required training sessions, whether online or in person, replying to texts and social media, lead generation, and then the potential for a personal unexpected call that your child is sick and needs to be picked up at school. All of these tasks often need to be considered or completed daily, as well as the expected number of actual sales calls required today. Time to get organized. We'll come to that topic soon. Even after you become an effective planner you will very likely need to occasionally alter the plan and continue to hone that skill forever.

Planning processes can take on a plethora of sub-titles. Planning breaks your tasks into small bites rather than a huge smorgasbord. Depending on your sector, you might start with your customer list, breaking it down by geographical location to ensure you make more calls per day. Your plan will include what time you get up each day and how your day is laid out. I typically started my day by 6:00 a.m. so my home office time was productive and I was still out the door by 8:00 or so. My first discipline is to review my entire day and ensure I am well planned for each call. If there are any last minute tweaks to the plan, I do that now. If you're a realtor, your plan will include looking at new listings and seeing which ones match your customer's needs. If you are selling automobiles, trucks, or farm machinery you may have just received a trade in and have a customer that fits the bill perfectly. Certain selling sectors will require follow up on every quote completed the day before. I typically use the first hour or more each day to accomplish this. I also check in the CRM to track my daily sales vs my budget for the month. You will never invest 100% of your time to an actual selling process. You cannot sell until you plan the process. Conversely, you cannot (or, at least, should not) spend all day planning and not get to the task of selling.

Every Sales Professional must know their product well. You must therefore plan study time. Whether selling houses or a security system, food, insurance, electrical wire, or pneumatic cylinders, you want to be as well prepared as possible. You won't know everything on day one, but your goal is to remain on a continuous improvement trajectory. Keep studying and asking questions. Get comfortable asking your customers for assistance, information and insight. They can become a key resource for your growth.

Early in our marriage we were looking at homes, but we didn't have a realtor who we knew or trusted, since we had just arrived in the city. We saw an ad for a nice country property and arranged to meet the listing agent on site. He had not seen the property himself and didn't ask us any questions regarding our needs or desires. Within moments of our arrival we knew the house required more work and investment than we were prepared for, but the agent did his best to hold our interest. He was new to the industry and was struggling badly to present anything positive regarding the dilapidated structure. At one point, he opened a door that allowed us to look under the house. He became very excited and said "Look at those beams. Wow, look how nice and straight they are." We laughed pretty hard once we returned to our car. He never asked for our feedback or asked what we were actually looking for. We made two calls with him—first and last.

If you initiate the sales call, you need to know the purpose of your call. Many times, my first call was merely to introduce myself and the services provided by my company. I did not necessarily plan to sell anything specific on that call. Instead of serving as a sales call, this is a rapport building call, and includes a strategy to extract information, allowing me to plan effectively for future calls. If, by chance, I perk his interest and he asks if we sell LED lighting for parking lots, then I had better be ready to present the options. I have been fortunate to work for large corporations that had a great piece of marketing literature depicting products we sold. If time permitted, I would certainly run through the marketing literature quickly, and watch for body language that depicted interest, or I'd ask if their typical buys would include this product.

It is equally critical to ask all the necessary questions to ascertain what homework you must do to ensure a productive follow up call. A realtor will need to know where the buyer wants to live, what area of town they may want to avoid, and whether they're looking for a one story bungalow, two story brick home, or a lakefront property. Price points and budgets often direct the conversation. If your client is buying a boat and has a $50,000 budget, he's likely seeking a newer boat. Does he want a pontoon style or a speed boat with wicked horsepower for pulling skiers? If you're insuring a person, business, or property, your planning process will involve gathering a plethora of data in effort to present a product that matches needs. Effective planning ensures all parties feel that the time invested reaped a healthy ROI.

There are a myriad of ways to find out more about the company you'll call on today. Initially, you'll need to find the street address and phone number, and, if possible, names and positions of key decisions makers. You may be planning to meet the procurement manager, the president, or another decision maker. You will research the annual revenue and earnings, number of employees, number of locations, any new announcements made regarding expansions or large contracts they have just been awarded, company vision statement, and key markets served. Finding out all you can will provide for better planning and preparation for that first call. He or she will be impressed to hear you came well prepared. Your extra research can also provide conversation points if time permits.

Let's assume you have a loyal customer who you've been seeing regularly. Does that alter your planning process? Absolutely! Your plan needs to have a greater focus than that initial call. The customer has now welcomed you to return, which in itself is a buy sign. It doesn't guarantee that the customer *will* buy, but the fact you were invited back opens up opportunities. Ensure that each call is now even better planned. ***You now need to know specifically why you are meeting.*** Be certain you are well-versed on the topic or products discussed, and ensure you are aware of the price and value. Prepare your open ended questions, allowing the customer to tell you what they deem important. If possible, bring literature or brochures on the specific product, or, if the product is small enough, bring along an actual sample. Bringing a sample allows for a quality check and other aspects the customer may have interest in. ***Do not assume a healthy relationship provides an invitation for complacency or mediocrity to creep into your selling process.***

There are many decision makers in most organizations, most of whom have limits or variations as to the dollar amount they are authorized to spend. In the sectors I sold to, the buying decision was often dependent on the department I was planning to see and sell to. I often referred to these departments as levels of government. Industrial plants often had a plant manager, maintenance manager, electrical or mechanical supervisors, procurement managers, and other department managers. Somewhere, there was a CEO, owner or president. My first target would be procurement staff and maintenance personnel. Many successes occurred where the person I initially met would introduce me to another who would be the key decision maker for my products. Other times, the person stonewalled me from meeting anyone else, stating that others would have no need for my products, or that their needs were being well looked after by my competitor. If the person shutting you out is a person of influence it is dangerous to go around them to seek out another buying influence. If it's discovered you went around them, you might burn a relationship bridge and future appointments may never occur.

You might initially think "Why not start by meeting with the president?" since everyone takes their orders from above. This certainly sounds like it would make sense, but it can be very challenging to get your first appointment at a new customer with someone as high-level as the president. Once you are in the door and doing business, it is impactful to inch your way up the authority ladder, each time ensuring no bridges are burned behind you. I advise you to ask somebody who trusts you to introduce you to the next level of authority. Rest assured that at some point, the company will need to spend a large amount of money, and that purchase order will need to be signed by the president or someone near the top of the organization chart. If he or she doesn't know who you are, has never heard your name, has heard no positive feedback regarding your top grade services and products provided, politics will prevail, and you are in jeopardy of losing the order after doing a ton of work. If, by chance, you know the president through another channel or network, ask him or her to introduce you to the key people in their procurement process. The fact that the president endorsed you opens all the doors.

Regardless of the product you sell, there will be a key decision maker in the group. If you sell real estate, you will need to assess which of the partners viewing the home has specific 'gotta have' features. One may demand a two-car garage, the other a modern kitchen with granite counters and a skylight in the ensuite bath. One might want an acreage where one wants a condo. Do not show them specifically what they stated they didn't want. You might say "I recall you saying you wanted a brick house but I have a new listing that is natural stone and stucco but has a pool and hot tub—and is in the area you prefer. Would you possibly like to see it on Wednesday while we're out that way?" This shows you were listening to their needs. It also shows that you respect their time, as well as the time of the listing customer and uses your time in a more productive fashion. If your customer demands a Dodge Ram, don't show him a Ford F150 without his permission. It just angers customers and can send them to another dealer and another Sales Professional.

Perhaps your company mandates that you make four calls per day. Others may set targets that include 50 face to face calls per month, but rest assured if there is CRM software in place, sales results will be tied to the number of calls made in person that month. Quality trumps quantity of course. The key is to target both. The harder and smarter you work the luckier you will be.

As you can see, ***planning and preparation is the cornerstone on which your success is built.***

Paul (Bear) Bryant, the Head Football Coach at the University of Alabama said "It's not the will to win that matters—everyone has that. It's the will to prepare to win that matters."

As a sales manager, I encouraged my teams to make face to face sales calls four days a week and use one day as a P&L Day (planning & learning). Fridays were my personal P&L day, where I reviewed the week, caught up on unfinished tasks, looked ahead, and planned the following weeks. I also did some reading on new products, perhaps completed online training, took in some breaths and rejuvenated the mind, body and spirit. Next week it starts again so be mindful of adopting a healthy work / life balance.

BALKTALK #2 – There is More than One Roadmap to Success.

A New York Times best selling author, Rory Vaden quotes "Success is never owned, it is rented. And the rent is due every single day."

If you watch PGA golf on TV you will recognize the name Bryson DeChambeau. He arrived on the PGA scene in 2015 and played his first pro tournament at the US Open. I am certain he planned well, practiced for thousands of hours preparing for that special weekend, yet he still missed the cut by four strokes. When he arrived on tour he weighed 205 pounds at 6 ft 1" tall. Golfers have nicknamed him 'the scientist' because of how precisely he plans his game and shot making. Most of us have golf club sets where each club is a different length and loft. Not him. He determined that he become an outlier and use a set of clubs that are all the same length. Most of us step up to the ball, maybe bend down and grab a few blades of grass, toss them in the air and decide which club to hit regardless of the yardage. Not him. He goes through a process that considers 9 different scientific calculations to assess which club to use. He even considers air pressure and humidity. During the COVID-19 lockdown he decided he wanted to increase his ball speed to 200 mph while most in the profession are around 170 mph. To accomplish this, he gained 40 pounds, some of which is muscle of course. He says he eats whatever he wants whenever he wants. His shirt size increased two sizes. He is a giant and is crushing drives 360 or more yards at times when he 'unleashes the Kraken' (the name of his driver).

Bryson decided there might be another way and maybe a better way to hit a golf ball, play the pro tour, and win. He thinks the game like no other and as one of his competitors said, "He puts in the work even when nobody's watching. He rarely fails because he never stops trying." As a Sales Professional, it should be your goal to have similar words said about you. Fast forward to the 2020 U.S. Open. Bryson won by 6 strokes and cashed a cheque of $2.25 million. He never gave up after missing the cut in that first U.S. Open in 2015. Put in the work, plan effectively, and never give up. Never stop trying.

So why did I share a golf story?

Your planning process might not mirror mine exactly but I encourage you to find the process that you can adopt—one that works for you, and one you can discipline yourself to try. If it doesn't work well, change it! Remember, if you do what you always do, you'll get what you've always gotten. Invest the necessary time in quality planning and you will differentiate yourself from your competitors. Your customers and clients will notice and reward you.

Don't get stuck in the rut of assuming there is only one way to success. A rut is just a grave with the ends kicked out.

2) Organized Focus

Your competitors will not be the barrier to your success. Allowing distractions to dictate your focus will be.

In my selling journey I have heard the word focus literally thousands of times. If you're a camera buff, you know you will typically focus on one key subject at a time, known as the focal point. If you're a hunter, you must focus if you plan to hit your target. When I was a kid my dad and uncle owned a marsh where they built a duck blind for hunting. I never had the patience to sit that quietly and focus on waiting for a duck to show up. Surely, the grocery store must have sold duck? My dad hunted pheasants too, so I walked what seemed like hundreds of miles through tall corn fields trying to flush out birds. It was wildly boring. I wanted to get home to shoot pucks.

As a Sales Professional, what is it you must focus on? Let's face it, none of you are volunteers. You were hired or promoted to your selling role to produce profit for your company. Out of that profit you will be remunerated. The more you sell, the more $$$ you make. In my selling journey, most jobs had a commissioned element. Because of this I would focus on selling the products that provided the most profit. The more profit = more commission. This may not apply to every selling profession, however for example, if you're selling cars, you might be paid more to sell a Corvette than a Chevette. Selling a million dollar home obviously reaps more commission than a $200,000 property. If you're in retail sales, you might be commissioned and make more on one product than another, or you might be paid a flat salary. Sometimes in retail the focus is to convince customers to apply for their specific company charge card. They know that many don't pay off the monthly balance, and they can end up making around 24% interest on the outstanding balance. Retail sellers do receive bonuses when selling charge cards, therefore must focus on doing so.

Focus does need to change throughout the day. On your first call, you might promote the product you know the customer needs, and later that day your focus might be on getting an appointment or selling a new product your company has asked you to promote. But while you're on that first appointment, stay focused on that goal. It can become easy for a busy mind to wander and rather than being invested in the current call, you might be focused on the showing of that million dollar lakefront property later today. Both are critical, and the fact is, that your career will be a consistent balancing act of selling many differently priced properties. Over time, you can specialize in selling a certain type of property, whether high-end condos, industrial properties, or apartment buildings. Set your goal and start moving toward it now.

You might ask "How do I stay focused with so much on my plate? My phone rings constantly. The emails are piling up. I haven't responded to calls from two days ago. I don't know what to do first." It is rare that a sales professional works alone. You may feel fully prepared to focus on what you were asked, and then your phone rings and your focus totally changes. ***Organized focus is a challenge you must become adept at, as it is critically important.*** A disorganized, scrambled mind is an unproductive mind. Focus is not simply tunnel vision. Though focus is necessary, if you're so focussed on one topic or subject you might walk through a customer's facility and not see the plethora of other opportunities you can discuss in ensuing calls. It is beneficial to think of the kind of focus you will learn, as looking through a wide angle lens at times vs a bow and arrow type focus other times. As you can see there are many types of focus. Organized focus is in effect multi tasking, where you ensure you hit your sales target today (pinpoint focus) while simultaneously noticing future opportunities (wide angle focus) with the same customer.

In effort to retain 'your' focus there are at least two actions you can undertake. Recall me stating that sales is a team sport? As stated, few Sales Professionals are running solo. Most are part of an organization that has teams I refer to as internal customers. Some call these people sales assistants, inside sales, or customer service agents. Regardless, you are not a soloist. You are in the choir. Though many customers might see you as the conductor, you know full well there are many assisting you on your success journey. As your plate fills, you must learn to delegate tasks and trust your teammates. They are there for this exact purpose—support. I stated in my journey of selling fluid power that initially I knew absolutely nothing of the terminology or technical aspects of that sector, yet won the National Chairman's Award in my first year. The inside support team was the key to that success, along with the enormous assistance of my sales manager and other resources. There were times early on that I didn't understand the question my customer was asking so the creation of a quality answer was a bit challenging. I never once shied away from stating I didn't know but immediately found the answer. Don't ever just make up an answer. Get the correct answer for your client or customer.

Actions to getting organized

Successful delegation is the first action to help you get organized. You cannot do it all yourself. Ensure that the person you've asked to assist you accepts the ask. It is exactly the same as a relay race where a baton is passed to the next runner. You must pass it, not throw it. They must accept it, not drop it. Once the baton is successfully passed, you need to keep an eye on the runner and hope they don't fall or drop the baton. An effective Sales Professional need not complete every task asked of him by the customer. Your role and responsibility is to absolutely ensure the task is completed with quality, and that your customer is 100% satisfied with the outcome or solution provided. Tasks are the baton in this analogy. *You don't need to run the entire race yourself.* How will you know what to delegate and what to do yourself? Time might be a factor as well as the perceived importance of the task. Trust is a critical ingredient to the delegation process.

Assessing the difference between important and urgent is the second action. As your business builds, the ability to manage a high number of customers and demands will become overwhelming unless you become effective at this assessment. Your customers will all consider their request as urgent and assume their request is being moved to the top of your priority list. While it is your responsibility to respond and let them know their request is important, you may need to alert them as to when you can get to their request. It is a good idea to actually ask when they absolutely need a reply. You can also assess who is best to address the request based on the level of importance or urgency. An important task perhaps can be delegated to a support member of the team but do ensure that you are kept abreast of the task being completed.

An urgent task might be one you want to retain yourself. But if that request comes to you as you are about to walk into a pre-arranged sales call, the urgency will not be addressed 'by you' perhaps for an hour. You now have a decision to make. At the very least be honest with the customer with respect to when his request will be addressed. Your integrity is always at stake. While listening, you'll quickly pick on how urgent he thinks his dilemma is based on voice tone, pitch and perhaps his speed of communication, especially if you know the customer well. You should consider the urgent call a compliment to you. It is critically important to review the facts and state your interpretation of the request back to the customer. Don't assume anything. Ask more questions if you feel the customer left out critical details. If the issue is urgent and must be addressed right now, ensure the person who gets the baton recognizes the stated urgency. Tell the customer who you are passing his or her request to, and let them know that you will follow up as soon as you exit your pre-planned sales call. It also bears saying that some customers will consistently present their requests as urgent tasks. You will discover which ones will scream "wolf" over and over. Govern yourself accordingly.

At this point, the important and urgent needs have been assessed and addressed. Now, back to the focus of the day. At some point check back with whom you passed the baton, to ensure the customer is totally satisfied. Take a moment to call the customer to confirm he is 100% happy with the outcome.

3) Discipline

As a Sales Professional there are many ways in which you will need to show discipline. Funk and Wagnells describes discipline as 'Training of the mental, moral and physical powers by instruction, control, and exercise.' John Wooden, the Head Coach at the University of California, LA won 10 NCAA basketball titles in 12 years. He has a plethora of classic quotes. One states "Discipline yourself and others won't need to." As a Sales Professional, I agree with Mr. Wooden. I learned quickly in my professional life that I needed to be self disciplined to succeed. Over the four decades of my career, I have likely been a bit hard on myself to ensure I didn't need to endure discipline from others.

So what is self discipline? It is what all PGA professionals show. They don't get paid just for showing up like some professional athletes do. Professional golfers work extremely hard at their trade without being monitored. They hit 500 *more* balls or 200 putts when exhausted or discouraged. I once worked with a man who actually played on the PGA mini tour for 15 years, and then received a ring the size of a Stanley Cup ring for his PGA membership. He said he hit 1500 balls on the range every day and had to tape his hands to cover the blisters. Self discipline sees you carry on and keep going when the going gets tough. You still get up early, follow your work pattern, focus on your goals, plan effectively, make one more call at the end of the day, stay active physically, and monitor your food and beverage intake. Self discipline takes a firm commitment to your goals regardless of the detours and barriers that will come. Not *if* they show up—but *when* they show up. ***You must adopt a relentless pursuit of your goals.***

I categorize my failures into reasons and excuses. My grade 5 teacher, Mrs. Price made a point of telling me that my reason for not having my homework done was an excuse—not a reason. I recall being so humiliated in front of the class who laughed at the comment. I have used this memory to discipline myself when I don't feel like putting in the work. The results in your rear view mirror will depict a lack of discipline if you don't do so.

My rear view mirror depicts very poor self discipline in my life insurance chapter. I knew very little about the professional aspect of self discipline. This resulted in poor work habits. Stephen Covey had not written his book yet on the *7 Habits of Highly Successful People*, and though there may have been books written on that topic, my excuse is I didn't try to find the keys. Selling success in my early career came somewhat easy, but I can now see that I may have adopted a thought process that I didn't need self discipline to succeed. Wow—was I wrong.

With COVID-19 altering many of our lives, working from a home office has become what many think is a temporary measure (though I think will become a norm for hundreds of thousands.) Working from home requires an extra measure of self discipline. As a Sales Professional working from home, you must develop high octane work habits and disciplines. Continue to get up at your usual hour, get dressed professionally, and put in a full day's work. When I was in sales management, I had a private office in my home. I needed that discipline of a professional atmosphere with all my diplomas on the wall, laptop, printer, library filled with sales books, photos of golf and hockey stuff, and, most importantly, pictures of my wife and daughters. Even on days when I assumed I would be at home all day, I would dress in my business casual wardrobe so I actually felt like a Sales Professional. For some reason, I seemed to perform better when I looked the part. I recall a hot and humid Friday afternoon with all my family splashing and laughing in the pool. My office faced the 2 acre beautifully treed backyard and I could hardly wait to join them. At one point, one of my daughters came to my window and said "daddy when are you coming to swim?". It was 4:30 pm and yet I knew I was paid until 5:00 and that is when I joined them. My self discipline would not allow me to swim before the end of my day.

Develop areas of necessary discipline whether it is sleep, exercise or constantly ensuring your trajectory for self improvement is on the success curve. Do NOT flatten this curve! Be honest with yourself. Not everyone finds this an easy task. If you're new to selling, you might not have yet realized how much self discipline it takes to succeed. If you know you will struggle in this area, ensure you find yourself a mentor to be accountable to. That might be your sales manager or another colleague. Ask them if you can meet weekly to discuss how each of you are doing along the journey you are on, regarding self discipline. Perhaps you are a strong closer and she is extremely self disciplined. We know it takes 21 days to create and commit to a new habit. Adopt self discipline. Once the habit is formed it will become second nature. Lou Holtz, a hall of fame college football coach stated "Without self discipline, success is impossible."

4) Executing

No–this is not what happens when you don't hit your sales budget this month! To execute is to successfully create, follow, and accomplish a plan that results in successfully achieving the goal you set. Sales Professionals have some of their goals set for them by management. It could be sales or unit volume, or profit goals. Whatever it is, you must be certain to discipline yourself to ensure that the actions taken will result in your best opportunity to execute the plan. I am a sports nut and have played a lot of hockey. I have heard a coach say "We failed to execute on the power play tonight—why is that?." We already know how critical it is to have great plans, and we know we must focus on the targets and goals to be disciplined in the actions taken to achieve success. But if we don't execute the plan we experience failure.

Most companies will expect a quarterly plan to be created and executed upon. If after Q1 of a fiscal year you have not reached at least at 25% of your goal, there is a risk of failure. At this point you may need to revisit your plan (step one) to see whether there are any tweaks that should be made. Once the corporate plans and budgets are in place it is highly unlikely your personal budget will be recalibrated. Always be looking at your business funnel to see what is going to come to fruition in Q2 as this could see you get caught up and back on track toward budget. We will cover funnel management later, as this is a critical tool for assessing your chance of executing your plan. If you need to change or alter your plan do it after Q1. This is not necessarily changing the numbers but perhaps your process and your focus. Always seek guidance from your superior. It will show him or her that you are aware and not hiding from the Q1 results, but are in tune and wanting some guidance as to how to get back on the path to the successful execution. Typically you will be remunerated based on the 12 month window, but even if you create a great plan, it may not result in wild success in year one. Your plan of execution might be great but your implementation might need more practice. Perhaps you have a great presentation but your presentation skills need some polish. You can improve that by disciplining yourself to practice. Don't get discouraged if your plan doesn't result in a great execution immediately. Great plans usually result in great results if you stay disciplined and focused.

5) Time Management

You will recall the myriad of tasks I discussed in the planning stage that could be required of you each day. Now, how can you possibly find the time to do it all?

Many people often cite "I don't have time for that" as a reason for not doing something. I personally have found that I always find time for the things I want to do or find value in doing. Recall we touched on the difference between important and urgent? Read that section again. It impacts your time management skills while navigating the 8 or 10 hours a day many Sales Professionals invest into their success journey.

I am a task-oriented man, and I always have a to-do list at my fingertips. Some of those tasks are important, some can be delegated, some done when I get to them, and some are urgent. As an effective multi tasker, you can get several balls rolling at once and allow each to come to completion as they do. Some will have a deadline like a government quote due at 2:00

pm. If it's late it will not get opened and your chance to succeed is zero. Others are urgent but may not have a time and date stamp involved.

A simple methodology for ensuring time is invested and not wasted is to only work by appointment. Your doctor, dentist, financial planner, and lawyer only work by set appointments, and you should too. It ensures that both or all parties involved are committed to the time agreed upon and are expected to invest that time uninterrupted. I can say for certain that my phone is shut off when I enter a selling opportunity. That shows your customer that you are grateful and respectful for their time. Your ringing phone could derail an important conversation or sale.

Sending a formal email meeting request is a great timesaver. It assures that the client has accepted the invitation, it sets a timetable for the call, introduces the agenda and makes it official. Sure, this can all be accomplished with a normal email and texts, but an accepted meeting invite is added to each person's calendar then provides an additional reminder 30 minutes prior to the meeting. I have at times shown up for a meeting and had the client be called away or worse, found out he or she forgot the meeting entirely, even with the reminder. Emergencies do occur, however, and we need to be understanding and accepting when that happens. It is part of being a professional.

Finally, at the beginning of the call, be sure to state the purpose for the call and the subject matter that will be discussed. Doing so sets the tone and direction for the meeting. It advises the customer that you have come well prepared. Productivity and time management is at the top of everyone's list these days, and providing the purpose for the call allows everyone to invest time wisely in hopes of a healthy return on the investment for all parties.

There were times in my Professional Sales journey where my sales territory was massive. My last role saw my furthest customers 5-6 hours from home, while many were 1- 3 hours away. Time management was a critical factor in ensuring my key customers were seen often enough that they knew they were a focus for me and our company. I personally found that geographical quadrant management was an effective way to manage large territories. It often required hotel stays, but my goal would be to see those in the 4-6 hour range at least once per quarter. The plan could always be tweaked, but it typically worked well for me.

In my Professional Sales journey my typical work week would be around 50–60 hours. I attended a seminar recently that stated everyone becomes increasingly ineffective after 55 hours and one man at the seminar estimated he worked 70 or more each week. When he spoke of his degree of stress and the impact his work had on his personal life, his emotions were raw. He was exhausted mentally and physically. His commitment to his job was putting his health and relationships at risk. Find a balance that protects both, yet promotes success.

Our most important asset in life is time. We can make more money but we cannot make more time. We must invest our time wisely, as it has a far greater impact on life enjoyment than money does. Our work-life balance impacts on how long we live to enjoy the money we make. Working 70 hours a week and making gobs of money and being buried at 55 makes no sense whatsoever. There will be no bronze statue of you built on the front lawn of your employer when you die, so it's important to get your priorities right, early in your career.

So, how do you manage your time? Adopt the term 'closest to cash' and accomplish those tasks that will relate to the achievement of your goals. Delegate the tasks that do not, and follow up on all commitments made to clients and customers.

It is interesting to look at how the management of time has become far more productive with the advent of Skype, Zoom, Microsoft Teams and GoTo meetings. I think the COVID-19 pandemic is going to make us all a bit more productive in some ways. Even prior to COVID-19, I often met with my financial planner via GoToMeeting, and I recently had a doctor's appointment in a similar manner. During the life insurance chapter of my life, all meetings were held at the kitchen table of the client, usually in the evening. Financial planners today typically work daytime hours and meet in their place of business. This way, they have less windshield time, can book back to back appointments throughout the day, and be far more productive overall. Yes, things have changed. During COVID-19, realtors have done virtual tours of homes and properties and again have had an impact as they work from home for parts of their day. Even my daughter was teaching her students virtually during COVID-19.

Realtors have tools at their disposal that save enormous amounts of time. The initial interview exposes all of a buyer's desires in a home. All that data is loaded into a profile and anytime their criteria matches a listing, it's emailed to the buyer saying "Len has a listing for you". Compared to the phone calls and car trips that occurred when I was first buying real estate, it is far more efficient. We could spend days driving from house to house and potentially wasting time for all parties. Efficiency has been created by technology but I have to say that at times I still miss hearing a voice and seeing my professional seller face to face.

6) Quality

It may seem foolish to say that we as Sales Professionals need to talk about quality. We all know we must deliver quality, yet in my journey I have experienced both sides of that coin either from internal customers and suppliers or agents in the industries served. If I am honest I likely took a shortcut or two in my day in effort to increase the quantity of work accomplished or over served some customers when one less served would have resulted in a few receiving higher quality work. I once had a manager who had a saying which was 'dirty feet'—DIRTFT—"Do it right the first time." Every parent on earth has made this comment to their children yet we still need to hear it as adults. Even today, I can catch myself tempted by a shortcut but I've engrained in myself that it's more important to do it right. We feel good when we do things right. That is what quality is.

Only sell products you believe in. That way you sleep well and can be almost certain there will be no awkward buyer's remorse conversations following the purchase. It can certainly occur that a product you like, believe in, and enjoy selling comes up with a bad batch just as some believe automobiles made on Fridays have issues. If, however, you start to see trends regarding substandard quality, shy away from selling that item or product. It will simply result in time wasted, and you'll be chasing warranty and replacement of the product. In the industries I worked in, some customers wanted to be remunerated for their labour to take down and reinstall a failed item. This always resulted in awkward conversations.

Let's face it: sales people have been given a bad rap for decades. I have been part of the sales circus for a long time, and have seen a few clowns. However, I would say most of those in professional selling sectors today, whom I have been associated with have elevated the flag of quality, integrity, and professionalism, and have done us all proud to be called Sales Professionals.

As a young or newer Sales Professional, you'll have many years to toil in the trenches, earning your respect each day based on your words, actions, clarity, and quality communication, void of ambiguity. No ear candy allowed.

4

RELATIONSHIPS MATTER

WE LIVE IN an instant culture. We expect fast food, faster internet, fast travel, and shortcuts to everything. Quality long lasting loyal relationships take time to develop and mature. Instant relationships are unlikely to endure the difficult days. Be patient. The wait will be very rewarding. I recently saw a plaque at a gift shop that read "It takes a long time to grow an old friend." I think this can be applied to most quality relationships.

We used to hear the phrase "people buy from people" nearly everyday. I admit to hearing it less often these days. Our world has changed. According to the U.S. Department of Commerce, 600 BILLION DOLLARS was spent online in 2019. In most cases, quick clicks on a smartphone or laptop result in the selling or buying of products. I also read that up to 40% of online purchases get returned. Wow! When online returns occur, you often don't have a personal relationship with your Sales Professional to monitor the process and ensure customer satisfaction. The COVID-19 pandemic has forced us to cancel flights and AirBNB reservations. Accomplishing that process online was a nightmare and was only possible by finally getting a human being on the phone.

In what I've referred to in this book as more traditional Sales Professional roles, face to face selling occurs often, which means you must develop trusting relationships. In these cases, people *do* buy from people. We all know someone who just has what I call the likeability factor. You meet them and something about them just says "we can be friends" or "he or she seems genuine." It's a magnet, isn't it?

Relationships will be critical to your success. They are also one of the most rewarding aspects of being part of the sales profession. Your relationships will enhance your network as you share your knowledge with colleagues and they reciprocate by introducing you to those within their inner circle. My wife and I have met and made friends through Rotary, church, new neighbours and charity organizations. When we moved to the other side of the country after 60 years in one province, we said "We can make new friends but we aren't going to make more kids." It was prophetic—we have new friends.

The bad news is that not all customer relationships develop the way you wish they would. Why is that? Did you do something wrong? Are you suddenly horrible at this aspect of your job? Are you a bad person and unlikeable? No! In most cases, that's not the problem at all! Don't listen to those voices inside your head. Sometimes you need to adopt the statement 'It is what it is,' and move on. Not every relationship is going to be equally rewarding.

There are many reasons some people simply don't gel. Industrial selling often sees a lot of competition. In fact, I suspect there is no sector without competition. However, some sectors see repeat business on a daily basis. In many cases, transactions occur daily between the same individuals, which is why it can often be comfortable for that association to continue.

Some customers are very loyal and you will come to appreciate that one day when they are loyal to you. Some customer relationships become personal where the spouses of those doing business become friends and the foursome socializes on weekends. Other customers might be extremely high volume having earned a rebate program. And, finally, maybe the current supplier is simply providing phenominal customer service, along with a solid trusting relationship. That's a tough one to break into.

I once met a potential new customer who told me he just had no need for another source. I thanked him for his forthright and honest answer and left. However, two years later, something changed and he called me to ask for a meeting. He became a long term loyal customer. It was therefore important that no bridge was burned during that first call. Professional conduct always pays dividends.

The important aspect of professional selling is to realize that there are hundreds of other customers, and you cannot serve them all. This is why it is important to build your relationships where reciprocity is appreciated. I call it the boomerang effect. When you do something nice or go beyond the call of duty for a customer or potential customer, it is natural human tendency to return the favour. Customers are people too, and though I have not always gelled well with everyone in my career, my findings are that most people are nice. They are moms and dads, sisters and brothers, or grandparents, each one coming to work on a daily basis doing the best they can for their organization. If they don't do business with you today, it might be tomorrow. Remain professional. Your day will come.

It is also important to recognize that not every customer is seeking a new best friend. Don't expect a dinner invitation. Successfully mixing business with pleasure can be challenging, but I have certainly experienced it. The challenge can come when things go wrong inside a business transaction. It then takes a pretty solid relationship to endure the incident that created the stressor. Effective communication and an immediate resolution to the problem can actually strengthen the relationship. Let the relationships develop organically and celebrate if you do find a new and loyal friend.

One might ask "Is it ever ethical to fire a customer?" Have you ever even heard such a phrase? My answer is yes, you can fire a customer under unique situations. If a customer intentionally sabotages your efforts or acts in an unethical fashion, then yes, I would break ties. There is no need for a showdown, but do feel free to walk away. If you are needing to make such a decision, the relationship is already at risk. When I was a branch manager, we had a customer who abused our Sales Professional by horrible name calling and language that was uncalled for. I too, had called on this customer to assess the situation and found it to be unbearable. I pulled our sales people out of the account and never called there again. Verbal abuse is not an equal exchange for money, and there are too many other quality customers to look after.

Each customer must bear fruit, just like an apple tree does. Fruit is profit. If a customer simply wastes your time and never buys anything, you will need to consider your return on investment. If they simply tap your knowledge and use your expertise for their benefit and then buy elsewhere, you will want to consider walking away. Customers who consistently don't pay their bills on time are those you will need to assess as well. I can only recall firing a customer twice in my life and each was with merit.

In another instance, I personally was calling on a customer who I knew required my products. He showed interest, and was always kind and cordial, but he never made a purchase. I decided to end my professional association with that corporation. On my last sales call, we had a very cordial exchange and this time I didn't make any sales pitch. Instead I said "This is my last call on you Henry and just wanted to thank you for your cordial welcome each time I called." He replied "What? Are you leaving your company?" I said "No, Henry, but I have been calling on you and presenting products to you for a year now, and I know you purchase these products somewhere else. I am sorry that I failed you in my pursuit of your business. I have not shown you added value and I apologize for that but in good conscience can no longer waste your time." Well he was absolutely floored and speechless. He asked me to give him more opportunity to purchase and did so regularly from that point forward. Neither of us ever mentioned that conversation again, and to be honest I never again used that strategy. It was risky and worked 100% of the time. Use at your own risk, but you must get a return on time invested (ROTI) with every customer.

As a Sales Professional be kind and as professional as you can be at all times.

Why? Because relationships matter!

BALKTALK #3 – Beyond the Call

While our two daughters were growing up, our household had a motto. You guessed it: 'beyond the call.' Any time they were asked to complete a task or chore, we asked them to do a better job than they thought we wanted or needed. As children, they certainly balked (pun intended) but as they grew, the concept seemed to sink in. As a family living on an acreage there were 2 acres of lawn to cut, a pool to clean (along with many other yard duties), plus household tasks their Mom asked for daily. When they were very young, we had a chart on the fridge that provided stars for completed tasks, which, at the end of the week determined their allowance. If they went beyond the call there was a bonus like ice cream at the Dairy Freez or a sleepover with a friend. When they hit the legal working age they each had jobs outside the house, one at an auto repair garage and variety store, the other at a grocery chain working the deli counter. Later, they both worked at a golf course as beverage girls, and being only 18 months apart were often confused as twins.

They had fun with that. Without fail, every employer would eventually meet their mom or I and ask "do you have any more kids we can hire?" Our eldest daughter worked that garage job for 8 years, through high school and university. At his retirement party, the owner claimed she was the best employee he had ever had. Our kids obviously embraced the practice and habit of going beyond the call.

Today, our two grown daughters, one an elementary school teacher and one a clinical audiologist, often speak of the motto. While we get some laughs from it, they quickly recognize in their own workplaces when others also go beyond the call.

As a Sales Professional, one of your mottos should be *'Go beyond the call.'* In our world of instant gratification, it can sometimes seem that shortcuts are the feast of the day. We have shortcuts on our laptops, shortcuts to get to work quicker, and thus it all can result in taking shortcuts to success. There will be many barriers and detours to that goal. Customers quickly identify those who go beyond the call, so be that person. Your reward will be customer loyalty, repeat business, respect, and a successful career.

Recommended book reading: 212 The Extra Degree—Mac Anderson & Sam Palmer

5

THE SUCCESS TRIANGLE

AT THIS POINT in your life you are now considered a consumer. You buy stuff. Perhaps you buy products from Amazon or Wayfair, but think about the times you buy products or services in person. Why do you conduct repeat business with that furniture store, clothing boutique, restaurant, or salon? Why do you take your car to be repaired at the same service center and potentially ask for the same mechanic who worked on your car last visit? Yes, you get to decide who to give your hard earned dollars to.

Imagine you have arrived at your usual hair salon for that great cut and colour, but on that day your hairdresser called in sick. You have a special occasion in a few days so you are assigned someone else to cut your hair. Chances are you aren't as happy as you typically are and we all know nothing grows slower than a bad haircut. Anytime you regret your buying decision, it's called buyer's remorse. I certainly have experienced it, and expect you have as well. *As a Sales Professional, it is your goal not to have your customers ever experience buyer's remorse, following a purchase from you.*

So why do you return to that particular place of purchase and seek out that specific sales person? It certainly is due to the previous experience being a favourable one, but it goes much deeper. Let's look at the success triangle:

KNOW

What does it actually mean to know someone? Who is your closest friend? How well do you know he or she and how well do they know you ; really know you? Hopefully we all have a best friend. The person who has seen the good, bad, and ugly, yet continues to be our friend. The one who hears your heart. I have a buddy who I have vacationed with often. We no longer live in the same province, so this takes some planning. We try to take an annual NHL hockey trip and have seen many games together over the years. Even after more than 25 years of being friends, we continue to get to know one another better. Your customer will only get to know what you allow them to know, and visa versa. Your role is to be known as a bonafide Sales Professional with the highest degree of ethics and honesty, great service skills, and as a person who is easy to do business with. There's no need to permit a customer to know you on a deep personal level unless the relationship morphs in that direction. Allow yourself to be well known and respected on the professional level. This side of the triangle deals with this aspect only.

Would someone buy from you if they didn't know you? Well, maybe yes, if you are in a certain retail environment, but I maintain that in many sectors the answer would be no. I have made purchases where I didn't know the sales person, but when it's time to make a substantial purchase I return to the professional seller whom I know. If you are in retail sales you will quickly find customers returning to your store and seeking you out based on their previous positive buying experience. I certainly saw this in the men's clothing stores I spoke of in my early sales journey.

Picture yourself at your customer's office. You have now made several visits. Do you know him or her? What do they know about you? There are many levels and layers to knowing someone. You might know 'about' their company. They might know 'about' your company but when does 'know' take root and start to result in business transactions?

Early in the business relationship, you know titles and responsibilities but until you know who people are on a deeper level, the triangle remains open. My suggestion is to be yourself. Let them get to know you. If the customer shares information about himself, he sends a message that he wants to be known and you may elect to reciprocate by sharing something about yourself. There are certain temperaments that take longer to get to know. Later we will discuss how to alter your selling technique once you discover your customer's temperament. An exchange of information is required to get to know someone. It takes time. Be patient. Nobody gets married after one date, and a customer isn't going to know you after one call. He could however decide he doesn't want to know you after one call. Maybe you failed to probe effectively, at the right pace, and maybe you went for the close prematurely and scared him off. You will need to read body language to discern how a sales call is progressing.

Obviously you can never get to know someone without many opportunities to communicate. I recall my daughter having a boyfriend in high school. I was occasionally a nosy Dad, and asked if she had talked to her boyfriend that day. She said "yes many times," but as I gently probed for more information, as only a Dad can, I quickly discovered she had not heard his voice at all that day. They had texted several times. I offered her some advice regarding communication which (I think) was well received. I maintain that once a relationship is well developed, texting can be an effective tool to confirm data, dates, and times but as your business relationship initially develops, you must be face to face to create the success triangle. Voices need to be heard. Faces need to be seen.

You will need to be the driver of the journey that allows the customer the opportunity to get to know you. This requires some sharing of information about who you are, where you're from, how long you have been with your company, how many years you've been a Sales Professional, and so on. You do only get one chance to make a good first impression: While some people are willing to change their perception of you, we all hear that "Perception is reality to the perceiver." If you get painted with a brush that says you are arrogant, overconfident, or cocky, you won't get a chance for your customer to get to know you, at which point the triangle could break down immediately.

Asking soft questions and listening intently will allow the customer to talk about himself. Everyone loves talking about themselves! Ensure you ask open ended questions that permit longer sentences. Be aware of your own body language. Don't invade personal space. Show a relaxed state of being as opposed to overly aggressive and ready to leap to the close. By gently and professionally extracting information about him or her, about their roles and responsibilities, about their tenure and company, you are deemed to be someone who cares about your customer, not just about the purchase order. While you are getting to know them, they are getting to know that you listen, and value their input. You will be the type of professional seller they want to get to know.

If you take a genuine interest in your customer as a person and actually invest the necessary time into the relationship, you will get to know them, at the desired pace of play, while they get to know you. The more you communicate, the better you will get to know your customer's styles and preferences, and the more the customer gets to know your level of customer service. Let it simmer and marinate slowly. It is worth the wait.

LIKE

Will a customer buy from you if he or she doesn't like you? Do you give your money to those you don't like? Stop and really consider if there are those whom you would simply never buy from and why you developed the dislike. There is usually a story that goes along with the decision.

I suppose we can all be a bit petty at times. We can refuse to give a person the benefit of the doubt, or jump to a conclusion that eliminates someone from our buying circle. But what if your customer doesn't like you because of some little thing you did, or didn't realize you did? What if a false accusation was made about you behind your back or a rumor was spread without cause or fact?

Did you marry the first and only person you ever dated? I know some can yes to that question, but for many that blessing wasn't as seamless. We dated, we liked or disliked or we liked and the other party disliked. Just as in dating, your business relationships will be more mutually beneficial and rewarding when both parties like one another. However, as a Sales Professional, the customer must like you first. You also are going to make a snap decision on whether you like the customer upon first meeting.

Let's assume for this moment that the playing field is level and nothing has occurred to jeopardize the opportunity for you to be liked. We all want to be liked, don't we? This goes back to kindergarten and carries on today. It feels great when we are endorsed, accepted, respected, and liked. It feels horrible knowing that someone doesn't like us. We all know people that say they don't care about what others think, but I am not necessarily convinced that's true. I think of Don Cherry when I consider someone who never candy coated his responses, was certainly opinionated and appeared as though he didn't care whether he was liked or not. I'll bet he preferred being respected though. Many were sad when his journey ended with Hockey Night in Canada. I met him once, shook his hand, and was shocked at the size and thickness of his hands. He is a big man and a real soft teddy bear. He was often brought to tears when certain topics touched his heart. I think he liked being liked.

Let's return to the other side of the triangle. I cannot think of someone liking you if they don't know you, at least in the business realm. So what can you do to cause or motivate your customer to like you? How will you gauge the progress?

Think about what causes you to gravitate toward someone. Why do you like a particular person at all? It is said we assess people within 7 seconds of meeting them. How fair is that? Some people might initially appear a bit cold and rigid or shy and reserved. Are they bad people? How about the person that is overly sociable and invades your personal space within minutes of meeting you? Certain temperaments won't like that. So is he or she a bad person who will never succeed in professional selling? Be careful of the tendency to judge too early or too quickly. Cut people some slack.

Attributes that most customers recognize and like are authenticity, sincerity, and honesty. Most people (including your customers) can usually tell if you are someone they 'could like.' If you come across as overly assertive, there is a temperament that will retreat from an immediate 'like.' Be honest, be friendly, be approachable, and as small opportunities are provided, ***do what you say you will do***. This is so very critical. The unprofessional overcommits and underdelivers. Customers will never like you if the level of service is substandard. From your first sales call, you need to check all the boxes to allow the opportunity to be liked. Be professional by sending the email meeting invite, be on time, be friendly, wear a smile and be positive, be well prepared, ask appropriate open ended questions, listen intently, gather information, and follow through on all your commitments. Then follow up the call with an email of thanks for using their time to meet with you. These are all steps and actions that can set you up to be liked. Try being late, wearing shabby clothes, and only talking about yourself the entire time and see if you get a second appointment. I can tell shortly into an appointment whether the like-o-meter is in my favour. In time, you will learn to read body language too, and become equipped to measure how engaged and invested the customer is in what you have to say. Are they asking you questions? Does it seem they are sharing or shutting down in terms of information? Are they disengaged, checking their watch, shuffling papers, and sending you all the wrong messages? The clincher is when they won't grant you a second appointment. It happens to all of us though, so don't let it discourage you. Assess, learn, and improve. It's a journey without a destination.

Accept that you might not initially like the customer who then becomes a regular and loyal buyer. Perhaps your two temperaments don't click as well as another does. Remember, you don't need to be in love with every customer. The revenue from the one you really enjoy is the same as from one you might struggle to be best pals with. Take your time assessing others and disregard that seven second rule. Instead, allow seven sales calls to occur before doing an assessment. Afterwards, even if you don't really like him or her, continue on your professional selling growth curve and let this be part of your learning trajectory. Look for the good in everyone because everyone has a nice button. It is your job to find it. Make your button easy to find too.

I have a funny story about me being disliked, then liked and accepted. This occurred when in Cape Breton, Nova Scotia at a golf course which was at that time said to be the best golf course in Canada—The Highland Links. I was paired with two club members, a stuanch elderly couple, so we were a threesome that day. I was on the practice putting green when the two cooly announced I was being paired with them. From the getgo the couple was unfriendly and certainly unwelcoming. The first hole required a 180 yard drive to clear a large marshy area. I hit my first two shots into the marsh. Now considered my 5th shot, I just took a 5 iron and just got it onto some green grass. I saw them rolling their eyes and heard the rustling voices of disgust. I took an 8. Neither spoke to me on the first green. I was so nervous and embarrassed. By the third hole I settled down and began to par a few holes but there was still no exchange of chat going on. I attempted to have them engage in some small talk but to no avail. On the sixth or seventh hole the man asked my name. I responded, and he said "We have an apology for you." I responded "Oh really?" to which he said, "After what we saw on the first tee, I said to my wife, 'this is going to be a hell of a long day.'" I laughed it off, stating I agreed with his assessment. After that they both treated me like a son and by hole 18 had invited me and my family over for supper. I shot 83 and did not accept the supper invite. Obviously this is a very unfortunate and shallow way to value a person, simply based on golf skills. It is, however, interesting how someone's opinion or perception of us can be altered based on our actions. Be careful how you treat each person you come into contact with. You never know what position they might hold tomorrow and how their circle of influence can impact on your success inside their network. The man or woman working in the storeroom might be President one day.

As a professional seller, you will potentially have the opportunity to take a customer golfing. That 4-5 hours on a golf cart is an excellent way to get to know each other, and can often be beneficial to contributing or completing two sides of the triangle. While I don't recommend you get in the habit of appearing to be buying business with an overabundance or imbalance of social outings, a game of golf is a tangible way of showing thanks for the loyalty a customer has shown. I have attended many NHL hockey games with customers, enjoyed hundreds of meals together, and even done activities that involved spouses at times.

I have observed companies who annually take their highest volume customers on weekend fishing trips, Major League Baseball doubleheaders, or to PGA golf tournaments. My observation is that these displays of thanks have a dramatic impact on customer appreciation, and I believe the return on that investment is substantial. Beware that some companies don't allow for such activities and if so, respect the laws of the land. I once had a regular Tuesday morning progress meeting with a Big 3 automaker to assess the project progress and their GM asked me to stop bringing doughnuts to each meeting. Nobody was happy about that but I respected the request.

TRUST

There is a reason trust is positioned across the bottom of the triangle. I believe it is the base on which the other two elements rest upon. It is my belief that unless you are trusted, 'like' and 'know' don't matter much.

When was the last time you made a substantial purchase from a company or person you didn't trust? For five years I trusted a particular heating & cooling company to look after all my needs in that category at various properties. Their service was typically quick and as I used them more they would occasionally provide a price concession. Over a period of a year however, it seemed each time they came, they would suggest I needed a far more expensive solution than just the $89 checkup I had booked. One time the technician strongly suggested I should invest in a better $800 solution. This past spring, the same technician said I might need a new central air conditioner but upon getting a second opinion mine was said to be just fine. Over the five years of utilizing this company and rewarding them with thousands of dollars in preventative maintenance and repairs, my trust eroded based on what I felt was questionable conduct. I came to know their service technicians were bonused on 'selling up' extra services and I just felt an erosion of trust occur. As a Sales Professional I am okay with selling up when a merit or benefit exists for the customer, but presenting fear factors to get a sale is unethical so don't do it. It is 100% fine to present a good, better, best solution if asked for, but never attempt to scare or intimidate a customer into spending unnecessary money over and above a budgeted amount. I am also not a fan of limited time offers and claiming scarcity of a product unless each is factual. Obviously there will be times when each is authentic but utilizing either as a pressure tactic could negatively impact on the triangle.

Would you return to a restaurant if you got food poisoning following a meal or to a salon that butchered your hair? Would you buy another vehicle from a dealer who's service department failed you? No—none of us would repeat buying in either of those situations.

If the customer has come to know you, like you, and now trusts you, your door is wide open for decades of success. How is trust built anyways? By and large if you say what you plan to do then do what you said you would, your bridge of trust is gaining strength. You show up on time, you deliver the quote before it is due, and you return the call when you said you would. Additionally you resolve problems and involve others if you are struggling with a solution, plus you offer fair pricing and correct errors if they occur. Further, you show you can be trusted with confidential information and don't gossip, and you don't change the price even though you made an error which may have been painful for you. A customer who trusts you will likely send you referrals. We often hear that an unsatisfied customer will tell 10 people about the bad experience. It is usually wrapped around buyer's remorse and there could be an erosion of trust. Some sales sectors rely more on referrals than others. Many Sales Professionals rely heavily on referrals. I know an automobile Sales Professional who is in such demand he only works by appointment and people wait to see him. I am told he sells 300 cars each year. I have purchased many cars and trucks from him over the years because I trusted him. He always went beyond the call of duty, was fair, impeccable in his details, extremely well organized, was friendly and likeable, flexible and amiable, was honest regarding vehicle history, and would tell me when not to buy a particular product if he felt it would impact negatively on my trust and our relationship.

Rome and trust are first cousins. Neither can be built in a day. It will take many transactions between people before trust is truly built. Trust continues to build over years or decades, especially in sectors where repeated selling occurs daily to the same audience. If you tell your customer the box of widgets will be here tomorrow at noon, you'd better be certain and be checking at noon to see whether it arrived. If by chance it did not show up, then you personally should make the call to deliver the unfortunate news. Have a reason and not an excuse. Also have the solution. Trust is like lasagna and comes in many layers. A customer might trust you with a $1000 sale but not a $100,000 transaction today. A year from now when the triangle is tightened up, the $1,000,000 sale could be yours.

I return to deal with professional sellers whom I trust. I have completed multiple transactions with the same person whether purchasing clothing, shoes, sporting goods, vehicles or real estate. Once the bridge of trust is built, we simply don't want to risk starting again with someone else. I even order the same meals at some restaurants because I trust the chef to prepare it the same as last time. We are creatures of habit.

Some customers will take much longer to reward trust. It must be earned and never arrives gift wrapped with a bow on it. The harder it is to earn, the more valued it will be. If trust is easily granted it might be easily retracted.

Know, like, and trust—The Success Triangle. Start building today!

BALKTALK #4 – Become a Trusted Advisor

You are known, liked and trusted. The success triangle is closed up tightly. Now what? Where do we go from here? Let's be real—the triangle will build slowly with some and will be considered built with others. You will never accomplish a completed airtight triangle with 100% of your clients and customers. But keep building and be certain that you keep the triangle fully secure once it is complete.

Let's concentrate on the customers with whom you consider the success triangle completed. You have earned the right to be heard at this point. The next step is to recognize that you have become their first call when they have a requirement. You might start hearing from them daily or many times a day if in certain industrial sales sectors. Each successful transaction adds another building block to the bridge of trust. As you continue to meet and exceed customer expectations, you morph into becoming their trusted advisor. The customer is the one who decides—not you. The title might never be spoken aloud between you and your client but he regards you as his trusted advisor.

If you are a financial advisor, you handle millions of dollars for your clients. You are their trusted advisor with respect to their retirement. Together you build a plan that protects their investments, assesses their risk appetites, makes changes as they near retirement, and educates them on taxation changes and government impaction on retirement income. They might also assist with RESP's in preparation for your child's future educational needs.

Regardless of what you are selling, you could someday be selling to the children of some of the people you sell to today. Perhaps you already are. It is so rewarding to get a call and hear that you were recommended by a parent, friend, relative or another satisfied customer.

> You have become their trusted advisor. Congratulations!
>
> Recommended book: The Trusted Advisor—David H. Maister, Charles H. Green, Robert M. Galford

VOICE OF EXPERIENCE — Fred Vigneux — Store on Wheels (Selling frozen food and meat, door to door)

Q – What age were you when you began your professional sales career?

A – Early on, I was a support worker in the insurance industry, then had some income properties. At 27 I owned 4 pizza stores. I had them for 13 years before selling them. I was 39 years old when I truly started making my living as a Sales Professional, and for the past 35 years have been selling frozen foods door to door.

Q – Looking back, how well prepared were you for professional sales on day one of your career?

A – I had no formal training at all, but talking to people felt very natural. My Dad died when I was 5 ½ years old and my brother, ten years my senior, became my father figure and mentor. At one point he was selling vacuum cleaners and then windows. I watched him closely and learned how to sell from him.

Q – Talk about year one as a Sales Professional.

A – It was February 1985 and very cold outside, so when I say I made cold calls all day I mean it literally. I had zero customers and decided only to sell to people I didn't know just in case the product turned out to be of poor quality. I didn't want to burn bridges with friends and family. When starting out, regardless of what you are selling, don't focus on selling to family and friends because you quickly run out of both. Real selling requires you to sell your product to strangers. At the time, the company I was selling for had 22 sales offices. In that first year I set sales records and was named Rookie of the Year.

Q – Has discouragement ever been a challenge at any point? If so, how did you manage it?

A – Rejection is at every door in this business. My theory was that when somebody said no, they actually meant 'know'. They need to know what it is I am promoting and selling. I recall a time about 15 days into my career when I had not sold any boxes of meat and the day was drawing to a close. On one of my last calls of the day, I decided to drastically reduce the price simply to ensure I wasn't totally shut out for the day. That day I only sold one box but the next day sold 20. I have learned never to take rejection personally.

Q – What was/is your biggest challenge faced on a day to day basis?

A – Early in my career it was anxiety of the first call of the day. We didn't work by appointments so I was knocking on doors and hoping not to get a negative start to the day. Once I had a sale I knew the day would not result in a shutout. That encouragement kept me selling. Now I have two full time sales people selling frozen food door to door as well. Both employees have been with me for 25 years. Today I have so many repeat customers, that anxiety no longer occurs.

Q – What has been the most substantial factor to any success you have experienced?

A – Confidence in myself and in my products. I have a personality that people seem to like and once they try my products, trust builds both in me and in the products and they often become repeat customers.

Q – Has there been one key person who has consistently impacted on your success journey and if so how? Would you consider that person to be your mentor?

A – My big brother for sure. As stated he was 10 years older than me and really took care of me after my Dad passed away. He impacted on my entire life in a positive way and was my mentor.

Q – When you experience a successful chapter in your journey do you allow yourself to bask in the sunshine?

A – Yes, to a point—but only for a limited timeframe. Each new day brings new opportunities. The one aspect I am most proud of is that I have never taken advantage of anyone or any relationship in my career and have consistently maintained a high level of integrity. I have earned high levels of trust from my customers. Additionally, I have not lost any friends by selling them my products which is very rewarding to me. People seem to like me and trust me. That's a good feeling.

Q – How has selling during the COVID-19 pandemic changed or how has it impacted your sales?

A – My sales have increased substantially during the pandemic because some of my regular customers didn't want to leave their house and be put at risk. Instead of buying one box they might buy two or three to reduce the risk of having me or my other sellers at the door too often. We always kept our social distance and would drop the products off in the garage or front step and the customers would have our cheque ready in an envelope. At the beginning of COVID-19 we made more phone calls to regular customers to ensure they wanted to be served and were comfortable with our approach.

Q – Talk to me about your sales process. Selling meat door to door for 35 years is a significant success story.

A – Well on a cold call I ring the doorbell and step back 5 feet, just to give people their space and did this even prior to COVID-19. I say "Hi I am Fred from the Store on Wheels. I am in your neighbourhood today and would like to show you some of my meat and frozen food products". If they say they are a vegetarian, I tell them about my veggie burgers. If they don't eat red meat I introduce fish. If they don't like salmon I introduce halibut. There is never an objection I am not ready for. In my earlier days in the meat selling business I was the sales trainer for all the salespeople in that company and have continually honed my skills over the years. If it becomes obvious they have no interest, I leave with a friendly good-bye. Maybe next time I will send one of the other two sales people to see if he gets a better reception. There are lots of customers out there. Onto the next house.

Q – How many hours per week do you work?

A – Today I am semi-retired so I am working 12 hours actually out selling, plus maybe 15 hours in the office. In my career though when ramping up I worked 6 days a week for many years.

Q – What one skill set has had the most significant impact on your selling success?

A – I am a very friendly guy who has a gift of gab. I am honest and considerate and since I am selling a tangible product it is important that people recognize those traits. It really builds trust.

Q – What has been your most significant regret professionally?

A – Not getting into this business earlier. I had my pizza businesses in the early 1980's when interest rates were near 20% and while that chapter was good, selling food is a recession proof business, and repeat customers allow for relationships to develop.

Q – Talk about work/life balance challenges and how you navigate it.

A – Today my balance is far better than initially, however I always ensured my priority was family. I'd work 6 days a week but shut it down at noon Saturday and spend the remainder of the weekend with them.

Q – What key piece of advice would you offer to the person just starting a career in professional selling?

A – If they were in my particular business I would say not to sell to family and friends and only sell products you have full confidence in.

Q – What would the experienced Fred of today tell the young Fred of 35 years ago?

A – Develop the mental strength and capacity to handle rejection without taking it personally. Develop confidence and skill in handling objections. Be assertive and knock on one more door or make one more sales call before you go home today.

BALKTALK #5 – Celebrate Small Victories

We all like to tell the story of the big fish caught, or the long drive at the golf course, or the million dollar contract won. Major League Baseball hitters who are in the Hall of Fame didn't succeed 70% of the time. Ty Cobb had a batting average of 366 when his career ended in 1928 after 24 years in the majors. There are, however, dozens in the Hall of Fame with averages around 300 which means they failed to get on base safely 70% of their times at bat.

As a Sales Professional, your efforts will fail *at least 70%* of the time. Every sector has different tools to gauge success, but if we successfully negotiated 25% of our attempts in the industry I worked, that was pretty darn good. This data can be tracked in your CRM (customer relationship management) software if your employer has one.

So with only a 20-25% success rate, you'd better celebrate the times you do win. What is a win? It might be getting the appointment you targeted, or meeting the key decision maker, or making 5 great calls in one day, or actually making a sale.

Recall Fred who almost went an entire day without a sale then finally sold one box of meat after toiling all day long. That was a victory. I am sure he was close to giving up that day but made one more call and that is when victory arrived. Your victory could be recognizing that your success triangle is ⅓ built or realizing the customer does like you. All successes need not be wrapped in dollar bills. You will quickly realize that quality execution reaps sales, profit, and income, but many small victories make for consistent pay cheques. Throughout this book you will read other Voice of Experience interviews and consistently read that the successful Sales Professionals took some time to celebrate victories. They didn't take a week off and stare at their monthly report but they did recognize the need to bask for a short period—to marinate in the success—and then repeated the behaviour that contributed to the victory.

6

YOU'VE ARRIVED AT YOUR APPOINTMENT—NOW WHAT?

PROFESSIONAL SELLING REQUIRES that you adopt a process to actually bring a sale to fruition. If you miss a step in the process, you put the sale at risk. When reflecting on your own sales journey in one, five, or ten years, you're bound to see a lost sale or two based on missed steps in the selling process.

Prior to your appointment, you should have sent a formal email meeting request along with the meeting agenda and a specific window of time to present your product or service.

Before COVID-19, it was customary to shake hands with the meeting attendee(s) at the start of the meeting. I once had a junior seller on the team who had just started with our company. One day, we were out making coaching calls. During the first call, he had his sales books in his right hand and when it was time to shake hands he got so nervous and flustered he dropped his books. On the second call, he again carried his books in his right hand, apparently not recalling that first awkward moment. Prior to the third call we discussed that I found if I carried the books in my left arm, it allowed for a seamless start to the call. We both had a chuckle about it and the ensuing calls started smoothly. I do wonder how greetings will change in the post-COVID-19 era. I now outline the necessary steps of a successful selling appointment.

Find Commonality

Ensure you show a good level of energy and smile as you greet your customer. This immediately reflects your friendly demeanor and invites them to reciprocate their friendliness.

When I enter a customer's office for the first time, I do a quick scan to assess how I can create conversation around what appears to be important to him or her. I am always determined to find a topic of common interest. Typically, the customer decorates their office with family photos, a picture of a boat, car, or motorcycle, a sports trophy or a coffee mug with the logo of their favorite team, or a picture of their pet. I check for diplomas depicting their professional accomplishments, and will sometimes use that as a conversational base. *Finding an immediate topic to briefly break the ice is an effective method of finding common ground.* It might seem obvious for me to tell you to make eye contact when chatting. Yet many sellers find eye contact awkward and challenging. Be sure to maintain eye contact with the customer, changing the focal point occasionally, yet looking at him or her when they speak. Blinking now and again is important as well–just appear natural and comfortable. Take no more than 5 minutes to converse in this initial stage of the call, then move on. Take mental notes of the things the customer enjoys on a personal level, as it might open doors for you in the future. If you both enjoy golf, you have found one topic of commonality. Later that day when you are creating the customer profile, insert those notes along with the findings you're about to discover.

Confirm the time allotment

At this point in the discussion, it is now a good time to confirm that the customer has also reserved the time you requested in the invitation. You can confirm this by asking "Thanks again for setting this time aside Warren. Is 30 minutes still going to suit your schedule?" If he says that he has blocked out the time, you must not go beyond the window of time he granted you.

I once was on a coaching call with one of our more senior sales people, Harold. He had held many positions of leadership at previous employers, stating that he had done both my job *and* my boss's job. He was clearly uninterested in being coached and truly didn't like having a boss. But he did like to talk. On this particular day, we arrived at the customer's place of business and Harold began to pull catalogues out of his car's trunk. His arms were full, and he started handing me even more catalogues. I assumed he was looking for something in his trunk but when he closed the trunk, the two of us stood there holding 11 catalogues. I said "Hey Harold—what's with the library?" His reply was "Well, just in case this is the only time I get to see this customer, I want to let him know everything we do."

Based on Harold's strategy and the multiple catalogs, I was eager to observe how this call would play out. Unfortunately, he spent too much time gabbing about nothing, failed to confirm our time allotment, and began to showcase every single catalogue. I observed the customer about 35 minutes into the marathon, shuffling papers, checking his watch, looking at his computer screen, and then folding his arms. He had clearly lost interest. It became obvious that Harold was not catching the signs, so I took over the call and shut it down calmly and professionally, thanked the customer, and left. There was no time left today to complete the selling process. Harold was never granted another appointment by that particular potential buyer.

In the planning process of the call you should request the appropriate amount of time to effectively present your product or service. If you need an hour, ask for an hour. There have been times when I conducted something called a 'lunch and learn' where the presentation included lunch for a small group. In those cases, it is essential to finish your presentation in 35 minutes and allow for a Q&A session. Be certain to only take the hour you asked for. The employer will then permit this practice to occur again when appropriate.

Part of being a Sales Professional is respecting your customer's time. Your customer should recognize that time spent with you is a good investment of his time and energy. In many of my meetings, I adopted the practice of letting the customer know that our appointment is almost over with five minutes or so left in the timeslot. If, by chance, I did not have time to fully complete the presentation, I ask permission to return at a later date to finish it. There are times when the customer becomes so engaged in the presentation topic that he or she pushes the limits of the time allotment. On many occasions, I've experienced the customer say something along the lines of "No problem Greg, I have another 10 minutes" when they notice that you respect their time. When your customer sees you respecting his schedule, he or she will also be quick to permit another appointment in the future.

Reconfirmation of the agenda

At this point, you should review why you are at this call; though you already stated such in your meeting request, it's important to reconfirm the agenda to allow the customer to agree that the topic is still relevant and of interest. Once there is agreement on the table, it's time to get to the meat of the meeting.

You should plan your opening statement to allow for maximum engagement. For example, you can say something like: "Ms. Jennings, I stated in my meeting request that I will introduce a high-quality lighting solution for your employee and customer parking lots. In preparation for this meeting, I drove by your place of business last night after dark to observe the current light levels. Can you tell me what benefits would be of greatest interest to your company regarding a potential upgrade?" This line of questioning opens dialogue and invites her to tell a story about the current lights, the hours of operation, wattage, age, failure rate, escalating maintenance costs, and perhaps the annual cost of operating the fixtures.

Once you have a conversation flowing, you might add "I've come prepared to show you the newest technology in LED parking lot luminaires. The product is North American made, has a 50,000 hour warranty, provides 163 lumens, and will provide increased light levels, ensuring that your staff and customers feel safe while walking to their vehicles at night. The power consumed by these luminaires will save your company thousands of dollars in hydro costs. A recent installation over on Peter St. has seen an investment payback of 19 months. Their lot size is similar to yours as well. I would be happy to provide the address for you and provide you the name of the Manager of that facility should you wish to get his feedback on their investment. Perhaps you can drive by tonight to view the appearance and performance."

Asking open-ended questions keeps the conversation going and allows for an exchange of information. Please remember that *listening is more important than speaking*. Try to avoid planning your next sentence after just asking your key question, as you won't actually hear what was said. Epictetus, the Greek philosopher once said that "We have two ears and one mouth so that we can listen twice as much as we speak." Keep that ratio in mind. You need information in effort to provide the best cost effective solution and she needs data to make a buying decision. She undoubtedly has a budget for the project, so be sure to ask for that number. Determine when it is appropriate to ask who else would be involved in the buying process. She could be the sole decision maker but she could also be the gatherer of information, and two or three other signatures are needed. In that case, offer to meet with all the decision makers if you feel she won't be put off by that request. Their company policy could state she needs to get 3 proposals prior to a decision being made. You'll want to determine whether price, ROI, or other key factors are driving the purchase. It is important to ask when the purchase will occur. There are scenarios where a company is merely budgeting for the following year. While your price might be good for 30 days, costs a year from now could escalate based on a number of factors, including raw materials, transportation, and manufacturing increases. If you know this is a budgeting proposal, be certain to clearly state your proposal is an estimate only.

Prior to the call, note some questions to ask and refer to them to ensure you cover what you planned to in that specific call. I often ask the customer if he or she minds if I take notes. While I make notes, I take a look at my own pre-call notes. Customers like to know that you want to retain the information they are telling you. Note taking is the best method to show them that you are invested in their time and initiative.

Determine customer priorities

When you meet the customer for the first time, prepare to ask open ended questions to effectively determine how to assess their needs. An opening compelling statement could be something like, "Mr. Hendrick, I am committed to you and your organization. I will never waste your time and I will consistently attempt to add tangible value through a process of addressing your needs, challenges, and objectives." This is a serious statement, and if stated, you must follow through, depicting your own integrity and professionalism.

Knowing what your competitive advantage is, over your competitors is critical. This requires that you know your competitors well. I suggest you complete a SWOT analysis on each one. This quadrant study assesses your competitor's strengths, weaknesses, opportunities and threats. You should also complete one for your own company's offering to compare. Knowing your company's SWOT provides you valuable insight on where improvements can be made, in effort to allow your competitive advantage statement to have greater impact.

It is imperative you discover the customer's highest prioritized needs, who he is buying from today, and what other products he might be considering. Ask the customer what his or her top three priorities are, and confirm if they would need to be consistently met before he or she considers buying from you. Find your customer's trigger points. Some customers say that price is their top priority, but upon digging deeper, you find that they really want great value for their dollars spent. We all want to feel that the worth of a product matches the cost we paid. Your customer may also consider the item's origin of manufacture, warranty, brand name, credit terms, batch billing, history of operational excellence from Consumer Reports, potential letters of reference you might have about you personally or your product, colours and sizes, after hours service, weekend emergency numbers provided, and associated charges for weekend service, what the commission rate is for the transaction, what closing costs or transfer fees exist, freight charges, return policies and restocking fees, FOB point, and whether your company has a customer satisfaction guarantee. You won't be listing these potential areas of interest but ***you must seek out the customer's top 3 priorities in effort to address them effectively***.

I maintain that all customers will return to where their needs are met or exceeded; so be sure to ask why they consistently do business with the ABC Company. What are they doing right that draws him back and how did they cultivate such loyalty and trust? Who is the Sales Professional representing that company? How mature is the business relationship? I have found the toughest barricade to break down is when there is a long and loyal trusting relationship where the success triangle is firmly in place. When that is developed with your customers you will enjoy said loyalty as well.

Once he or she has shared their top 3 priorities, address each one individually with honesty. It could be that the customer says she wants the guaranteed lowest price. Perhaps that is an objection you need to address with a statement that focuses on the top notch quality of your product, and while it isn't the cheapest, it is the one with the best warranty and highest specifications in the industry.

Perhaps she cares more about a problem-free purchase. She wants to do her best to ensure she does not experience buyer's remorse. ***Have data on hand to support the stated quality of your product.*** If what you are offering is service, such as a realtor would, your commitment might be wrapped around the marketing plan for the property you are about to list. In this case, ensure that the initial list price is realistic to sell within a timeframe, and consider offering a planned price correction if no offers come in within an agreed upon timeframe. Prepare a listing of several other properties that are similar to his for comparison sake and discuss the commission rate. If your customer is asking for a good lawyer to handle the transaction, be prepared to provide that. My wife and I recently sold a property. Prior to listing it, our realtor, Evan Goode invited us to his office where we reviewed a professionally produced video on how they planned to market and sell our property. It was time well invested, and the property sold quickly within 1% of the listing price. We have completed several deals with this Sales Professional who will complete a Voice of Experience interview in a later chapter.

Provide a confident solution

You've asked all the critical questions and determined what your customer's needs and priorities are. As you present your solution, *__don't mention cost first.__* In some cases, there will be a melody of solutions that could address the stated need. Be careful not to confuse or overwhelm your customer with a shopping list of solutions. Certain temperament types become decision paralyzed by multiple options. I refer to temperaments (personalities) in chapter 8. Your customer trusts you to present a solution that meets the key criteria. Focus on his or her top 3 priorities. If you are embarking on a substantial project, be certain you know the budget, otherwise your solution could put you out of consideration. If your customer has a $25,000 budget for a new car, then the brand new Corvette is out. If they want a diesel truck with an 8 ft box able to pull a 38 ft travel trailer, don't show them a 4 cylinder gasoline truck. You can, however, show them a couple applicable options or makes of product. One might be newer with high miles or kilometers on it while there might be an extremely well kept older vehicle, extremely clean under the hood. Both are $25,000 so you now have presented two solutions which provide for a decision by your customer.

My personal preference is to present one solution I firmly believe in, providing it fits the customer's budget. Industrial selling can still open up multiple solutions, but if I am being considered the trusted advisor, I prefer to come well prepared and confident in my solution, along with documentation of other successes when using the product presented.

Gain Agreement on the Solution, then Ask for the Order

Your responsibility thus far has been to provide a confident solution that meets exactly what the customer has asked for. Providing you know the budget, your customer is trusting that you've not shown up with a $35,000 truck when he told you his budget was $25,000.

Start with the features of your product and match those directly to what the customer's priorities are. Align your delivery to stated need. As you run through the needs matching process, stop after each priority, and ask if that's what the customer envisions. This builds momentum toward closing the sale. If you've done your job, the answers will be yes, yes, and again yes. What you're providing is an easy low-stress process in which the customer decides to buy your product because he has no objections. You delivered everything he asked for. Why wouldn't he buy? Once you've met every stated need, *always ask if there is any detail you overlooked or failed to deliver on. If he or she says no, then it is time to ask for the order.* This is where many junior sales professionals get stuck—but without this necessary question the sale might stagnate. If the customer leaves or you leave his office, he might buy the next solution that comes through the door merely because he was asked to buy. You must close with confidence!

Now you've asked for an opportunity to finalize the transaction. Have you ever heard of the ABC of selling? **Always Be Closing.** While Sales Professionals recognize that we must seek to close the sale, be cautious about this concept. Be certain you have assessed the temperament of the customer before closing prematurely or too often. If he hesitates, feel free to ask what the barrier is, and if there's anything you can do to remove the barrier. It could be he just wants a day to sleep on it or maybe he has another solution in mind and now has a decision to make. If you are stuck in this place, your best option is to ask him when you can follow up with him next. Don't apply a great deal of pressure, because again, certain temperaments will run away. He needs to be confident that you did what you said you would do, and be certain all his criteria has been addressed. He'll be buying from you if you have met the know, like, and trust factors. ***Once you have an agreement that your customer is going to buy, STOP SELLING.*** Yes, stop talking and present the documents that allow for the finalization of the process.

While I'm often the seller, I'm occasionally the buyer too.

One day, my wife and I were on a mission to purchase a new dishwasher. We had shopped around and found the model we wanted. In our hometown there was a great appliance dealer who advertised the lowest price and would match all other prices. The sales person showed us the exact model we wanted and proceeded to speak about all the great features. He did not, however, ask us to buy the dishwasher. **He didn't actually ask us anything.** He just talked. Since he didn't ask for the order I thanked him and we left the store. My wife was very annoyed at my strategy considering the dishwasher was just the one she wanted. Eventually, we did buy it. Happy wife—happy life!

Five years later we had moved and were shopping for another new dishwasher. This time, the sales person upsold us from what we asked to see. The model he showed us was far nicer—a KitchenAid vs a Kenmore. It was also on sale, and admittedly a great value. As the salesperson explained the virtues of this stainless steel, ultra quiet machine, my wife stopped him and said "We'll take it." I didn't even get a chance to negotiate this time! My wife called this a win/win. We still laugh about this story. I won't be taking her with me to buy a new car though. Yes, always ask for the order!

Not every transaction is for $25,000. Perhaps it's a $600,000 house or a $1,000 roll of electrical wire. Each sale requires attention, but not every selling opportunity will require that every single step in the selling process be followed. Ensure you respect the customer's time and be flexible and astute enough to recognize when to abbreviate the process. There are customers that simply want their need met and you are their trusted advisor. They may need a price estimate but delivery of the product *today* is their number one criteria. Always be fair and loyalty will be your reward.

Last, but certainly not least, ***always thank your customer for the purchase they made.*** A quick email after the audible thanks will once again set you apart from other sellers who just take the sale and move on. A realtor I know sends a gift card or a bottle of wine following a successful transaction. You get to decide how to provide a sincere thank you.

To receive your free gift please go to www.gregbalkwill.com. You'll be thrilled with what you receive, relevant to this chapter.

BALKTALK #6 – Complete a POST CALL Self Assessment

As a newer Sales Professional you should carry a checklist of the steps required to get through your selling calls successfully, until the process becomes automatic. I have occasionally returned to my car following a sales call, disappointed in myself after forgetting a key element or step in my presentation.

No worries though—just learn from every call you make. You'll keep getting better. Find your own tricks of the trade that fit the eye of most customers. Start to learn about body language and assessing temperaments so you can alter your approach to his or her buying preferences.

There's nothing better than acing a sales call. Even if you did not make a sale that day, celebrate the fact you followed the process and the customer relationship moved within the triangle. Now you simply need to perfect the process, be willing to tinker with what works for you, and keep building your confidence.

You just got an A+ on that selling call. Congrats!!

7

DOES GOAL SETTING REALLY MATTER?

TO SUCCEED AS a professional seller, you must set goals. This is not optional! Many will not want to risk failure by setting goals. Muhammad Ali said "He who is not courageous enough to take risks will accomplish nothing in life." Succeeding long term in this career is not going to be easy, but if it were easy anybody could do it. You are not just 'anybody.' You are a Sales Professional! As a child, you probably had a goal of learning to ride a bike, and then to hit a baseball, or make that sports team at school. Perhaps you set a goal of being an honour student or even valedictorian of your graduating class. Perhaps your goal was to become an engineer, red seal tradesman, lawyer, teacher, or health professional. I have two highly skilled daughters—one an elementary music and drama teacher and one an audiologist. Without goal setting, neither would be in their chosen profession. What goals have you set?

When you set a goal, write it down and keep it in front of you daily—that forces self accountability. If you share your goals with others, you may feel accountable to them. Maybe you will be asked about how you are progressing toward that goal. How awkward is that? Imagine you're at Weight Watchers and want to hit a target weight. Each week you are weighed in, and the fact you are expected to attend and be weighed in causes behavioural changes throughout the week. You must discipline yourself to stay on track to attain your goal this week. Gaining one pound is not the goal.

Tony Robbins, one of our generation's most effective motivational speakers, states that people don't set goals so they don't have to experience failure. We all fear failure. Micheal Jordan said "I have failed over and over and over again in my life and that is why I succeed." Further, Tony says that decisions shape your destiny. Patterns lead us in a direction." Good habits, which take 21 days to develop, are key to attaining your goals. Tony then states that your mindset drives your actions. You must develop strong mental muscles in effort to stay focused on your goal. ***Your mindset will determine whether you keep moving toward or away from your goal.***

Now let's look more closely at ***SMART*** goals.

S–Your goal must be **specific.** The goal is not to lose weight. The goal is to lose ten pounds by June 1. The goal is not to sell more cars. The goal is to sell 15 new automobiles and 10 pre-owned vehicles by month's end. Your goal is to sell one house every month in the next fiscal year, or to sell 30 sets of hearing aids by month end. Why is this important? Read on.

M–Your goal must be **measurable.** Ambiguous goals cannot be measured. A goal that cannot be measured cannot be celebrated when accomplished. You must be able to look at your goal and state whether or not you hit the target, in no uncertain terms. If your goal is to make $500,000 in sales this month, you either hit the goal or you don't by the end of the month. Reset your goal for next month.

A–Your goal must be **attainable.** There is no point in creating an unrealistic goal and setting yourself up for disappointment. If selling 100 cars this month is unattainable then why make that your goal? On the other side of the coin, setting puny goals and hitting them every time won't provide much self satisfaction nor boost your confidence. Joel Osteen, a New York Times best selling author, states that if the goal doesn't scare him, it's not big enough.

R–Your goal must be **realistic.** Setting a goal and attaining it builds confidence and motivation to set new, larger, and more challenging goals. Getting a new house listing every day is not a realistic goal. Making ten face-to-face selling calls each day is not realistic. Making four high-quality selling calls each day is specific, measurable, attainable, realistic, and is time bound.

T–Your goal must be **time sensitive.** Your goal might be to sell 24 homes in the next 12 months. It could be to lose 10 pounds by June 30 and 20 pounds by Christmas. On that date you will have accomplished your goal and be able to celebrate having hit your SMART goal.

Say you're a Junior Sales Professional and you have become aware there is a Rookie of the Year sales award up for grabs. Your goal is to win that award. It is a specific goal. It is measurable because you will hold the award when you win it. The goal is attainable because the award exists and you believe you have the skill set to earn the award over the other rookies on the team. It is a realistic goal, because you know you can commit to good work habits, staying focussed, setting your mindset on learning, increasing your selling skills, and committing yourself to a self improvement trajectory. You will keep the goal on your bathroom mirror and in your vehicle, so you can see it multiple times a day. Winning the award is a time bound goal, since the award is based on your selling success in the calendar year. Yes! This is a SMART goal.

I recommended you set several goals. Some will be personal and some professional. Your goal might be to read one book each month on any topic. I have a goal of walking 10,000 steps each day, and doing my core strengthening exercise routine daily. Maybe you have a goal to pay your car off by a specific date, or to learn to speak a new language before your next vacation. You might set a goal of having a date night each week with your significant other or upgrading your computer skills at the local college. Having a few SMART goals is extremely healthy for your overall well-being. *To reach your goals you will need to be relentless in your pursuit of them.* You cannot set it and forget it. This is not a George Foreman grill. Keep them front, centre and highly visible at all times.

As a kid, I never learned to swim and I feared deep water. At 35 years old I was out boating with some buddies when they convinced me to try water skiing. I was petrified, but had a life jacket on, so I decided to give it a try. I did a soldier dive off the side of the boat and came up under the boat smacking my head. I was truly in panic land. I was scratching fiberglass, but eventually surfaced. Then, while trying to get the skis on, I ripped open both shins. I didn't end up getting the skis on, and accepted defeat. It made for some hilarious laughter for the three guys on board and for some embellished stories at the office the following day.

Because of that experience, I set a SMART goal to learn to swim. I signed up for a beginner's swim class at the YMCA, and, low and behold, when I arrived at the first class I found out that I was the only adult signed up. Many class members were 8 years old and younger. One of the moms thought I was the instructor so I had to fess up and admit to being a student. She was a bit speechless. At the end of 8 weeks I did earn my 'dolphin badge' along with the other kids. My SMART goal was achieved.

I then set a goal of ensuring my daughters would learn to swim early in life. We installed an inground pool and they both became lifeguards as teenagers.

BALKTALK #7 – Crusty Emails go to Draft

Believe me when I say that there will be times you will want to share a piece of your mind with a deserving recipient. Somebody deserves to be torn apart by some rabid articulation. Your fingers fly over the computer keys, you can hear your heartbeat, and your blood pressure spikes, yet it feels so good to get your rage out of the tips of your fingers. Yes: writing seething emails can be therapuetic. But when you feel compelled to act on this need, make sure that you do not type a name in the recipient area of the email. There is always a chance that as you spew out your frustrations, your finger might accidentally touch the 'send' button. It will be an OMG moment. Instead, if you must, go ahead and finish the email, put it in your drafts overnight or a couple days. Review it under cooler emotions and assess the wisdom in sending it. Ninety-nine percent of the time I have deleted the email. There were other times I typed and sent a frustrated email quickly and regretted the outcome, especially if it negatively impacted a relationship.

Take a breath. Save a relationship.

8

SELLING TO TEMPERAMENTS

EACH OF US has a personality. We rarely hear someone say "She has a wonderful temperament"; instead, we're much more likely to say "She has a wonderful personality." It's very easy to assess our children's temperaments. When my wife and I visited our daughter's grade 1 teacher, she stated "My, your daughter sure is a bossy little thing, isn't she"? I replied that a great leader is likely in the process of developing! My daughter went on to become the captain of many sports teams, and she now runs an audiology clinic. She was the only audiologist retained during COVID-19, and she handled all associated calls and issues for 12 clinics in the province. Her leadership skills have developed quite nicely and her sparkling personality keeps her clientele returning.

There are four key temperament types. I initially became interested in this topic when I was 19 years old. Later, I read a book by Florence Littauer called *Your Personality Tree*. After reading the book, I became deeply interested in why certain people were the way they were, why some were shy and others more extraverted, why some were always so competitive in sports, some more level headed or compliant. Later, I observed that some people were analytical and methodical, some more patient or restless. The study of temperaments is an important key to knowing yourself and knowing how to sell to those who are both similar or different from you. You know the old phrase 'opposites attract?' This often appears to be the case in personal relationships *and* in the selling profession. You will probably be more naturally attracted to customers that are opposite your temperament. You will, however, need to become astute at selling to all temperaments.

The four temperaments I was first introduced to are choleric, sanguin, phlegmatic and melancholy. Others refer to type A,B,C,D. Most of us are blends of two or even three temperaments.

Everybody knows someone who is said to be a 'Type A' personality, but few know what Type B or C is. While in sales management, I completed formal temperament assessment training at The McQuaig Institute, and became a McQuaig Interpreter. I found their profiles uncanny in their accuracy. I think it's scary that someone can get to know who they can expect me to be and how they should expect me to react under all professional circumstances. I utilized this hiring tool before hiring anyone and would confirm the accuracy of the report to ensure he or she agreed with it. The report would produce about 22 pages of data and I found it to be nearly 95% accurate.

McQuaig measure on the following scales:

Dominant ⇨ Accepting
Social ⇨ Analytical
Relaxed ⇨ Driving
Compliant ⇨ Independent

Behaviours in each quadrant determine how one will most likely react in certain situations. I was always hiring sellers so my goal was to pre-determine the behaviours of he or she in selling environments.

Let's look at the four temperaments:

Choleric – (Type A)—Typically a dominant, take charge sort who is a torid goalsetter, committed to seeing their goals achieved. They are savvy, analytical, logical and practical with a straightforward no-nonsense communication style. If you ask for their opinion you will expect to get their opinion—like it or not. They do not sugarcoat. The Choleric type's motto is 'let's get to work.'

When selling to a choleric, you must arrive well prepared. He has no time to waste nor does he see the value in too much small talk. He wants features and benefits, the value-added stuff, and will see through you quickly if you are shovelling nonsense or senses you don't know your product well. If his confidence or trust in you erodes, it can be a challenging selling journey here.

Sanguine – (The social butterfly–Type B)—Highly talkative, adventure seeking, enthusiastic, extroverted, charismatic, extremely social, and usually well liked by friends. They are quick to be a friend and make a friend, are very trusting, to the point of naivete at times. This person is fun to be around, will promise the world, but not always deliver. They might be late for appointments because they were busy or forgot. Details won't always matter but they are a joy to have around. Their motto is 'let's have fun.'

Selling to this temperament requires that you find commonalities. The sanguine type is immediately interested in having a strong and professional friendly relationship. They will recognize the features and benefits of your product if properly presented. Present your most effective solution or they will take forever to decide what best action they should take. This temperament requires proof, so a referral or testimonial is impactful.

Phlegmatic – (Type C) This is the most stable of the four temperaments. They are calm and easy going, a type that rarely blows up or has emotional outbursts. These are the observers in life. They are non judgemental and don't waste a lot of energy arguing and getting involved in disputes. They are classic introverts and are very comfortable spending time alone. The Phlegmatic motto is 'let's all relax and get along.'

Selling to the phlegmatic requires patience on your part as a seller. They won't be pushed or pressured into buying. They will perform their own due diligence, and will do their homework prior to making a decision. They want to get to know you first, so allow that process to evolve naturally.

Melancholy – (Type D) This temperament is thoughtful, reserved and self reliant. They are often seen as being perfectionistic, and detailed oriented. They are often dark, pessimistic, withdrawn, seeming sad or moody. They are likely serious all the time and rather unsociable. This is not a temperament that buying customers are typically drawn to. My findings are that the melancholy temperament rarely pursues a career as a seller.

Selling to the melancholy temperament requires that you deliver details, facts, and numbers. They need to know the benefits because they typically have a low risk tolerance and will take time to decide what they should do. Let them know the high degree of quality and accuracy you'll deliver. The melancholy type will buy your products once you have developed and earned their trust and can become a loyal customer.

Summary

I have coached several temperament types and have witnessed many temperament combinations excel in professional selling, so don't let anyone tell you only Type A or choleric, dominant drivers excel in the selling arena. Type A types seem more naturally driven toward goal setting and achieving results, but a methodical, analytical seller doesn't miss the details, is often more observant, and sometimes delivers a better product in the end.

The phlegmatic seller might study and perfect the sales process, but risks becoming overly rigid, insisting on following the exact process at each and every sales call. There is a risk that he loses customers' interest, especially if he is selling to an impatient choleric.

The sanguin seller wants to be everyone's friend but might overlook the customer's signs or body language. Most people and most sellers are a blend of these types, which means that nearly all temperament blends can succeed in professional selling, providing they know their own strengths and weaknesses and can learn to assess their customer's temperament as quickly as possible and sell to his buying style.

There are many online tools you can utilize to assess and determine your own temperament type. Doing so can be both fun and interesting! The better you know yourself, the easier it will be to sell to those of your own temperament and the other temperaments outlined herein.

Failing to assess a customer's temperament can have significant consequences. In one scenario, I provided a customer with several product samples to be installed on a machine in his stamping plant where car hoods were being produced. I followed up a few times to ask how the product had performed and each time the customer stated he had not yet installed the product. I pressed on, ignoring and misinterpreting his temperament. He was a quiet soft spoken man who was always cordial and friendly, yet he seemed to struggle to move in the direction I preferred. On yet another follow up sales call, my samples were in a box on his desk. He said he no longer needed them. He had purchased an alternate solution. When I queried him on why he selected the alternate method he told me straight up that I had applied too much pressure and he didn't like that style of selling. Wow—what a kick in the gut that was! Here I was, a guy supposed to know how to assess and sell to all temperaments, but in my choleric (Type A) haste I simply failed this time. This provided a valuable lesson though and sent me back to studying the four temperaments.

BALKTALK #8 – Skilled Sales Professionals Can Sell Anything

You've read that I have sold many products in my sales journey. While I didn't actually see myself as a sales person at nine years old, my sales skills slowly developed to where I am now, having successfully sold a myriad of products and services. Once the training and years of experience are behind you, you can sell anything. Your 'skills' are transferable. You will hear people say "she has great people skills." We might assess that she is a friendly person, but it goes far deeper. Those words likely mean that she is a great communicator, has a friendly temperament, shows genuine interest in others, and asks open-ended questions about their life. Other skills will reflect that she's a great listener, keeps her commitments, loves solving problems for customers, has a passion for selling, and has high ethics. Once you have developed many of these traits and skills all you truly need is product knowledge and training. Recall when I knew absolutely nothing about fluid power yet with my selling skills married to the technical prowess of many others, the team succeeded. Over my 10 years in that sector I learned an enormous amount about fluid power, but cannot say I ever became an expert. However, the experts joined hands with me to assist in the success journey.

VOICE OF EXPERIENCE — Tim Wilson — Partner at an Insurance & Financial Services Co.

Q – How old were you when you began your Professional Sales career?

A – I had many part-time sales jobs and as a kid: I sold the TV Guide door to door then later worked in a shoe store. At 27 I entered the insurance industry and became a partner at 34.

Q – What were you selling at that point in your career?

A – Commercial, business, and manufacturing insurance.

Q – How many years have you been in Professional Sales?

A – 23 years in the insurance sector and continuing today in some other interests and business ventures.

Q – Looking back how well prepared were you for the selling aspect of your career on day one?

A – Woefully unprepared.

Q – Talk about year one as a professional seller.

A – There was overriding fear. I had a desk in the back office area and hearing steps coming toward me created anxiety as I feared they might see me as an imposter.

Q – Has discouragement ever been a challenge? If so, how did you journey through it?

A – Of course it has. It is a constant battle and comes with the turf in sales. It's the seasoning in the stew. My constant companion. It is crucial that we deal with it though. I refer to the movie Cinderella Man where he simply did what he had to do. He had no choice and

I felt the same. I had no plan B. I felt that this gig (insurance) has to succeed.

Q – What was/is the biggest challenge you faced on a regular basis in selling?

A – Well—after fear, I was too easily influenced by others' opinions. I functioned below the surface of life and learned to work confidentially and quietly, not allowing others to know what I was working on or what business initiatives I was involved in.

Q – What was the most significant factor to the success you obviously have had?

A – Grit and Perseverance—and functioning despite the fear. I imagined in my mind that I was confident and smiling on the outside and adopted a 'go for it' attitude regardless of any barriers.

Q – Has there been one key person that has consistently impacted on your success journey, and if so, do you consider that person to be your mentor?

A – No.

Q – When you experience a successful chapter in your journey do you allow yourself to bask in that sunshine?

A – Yes, but only for a fleeting moment—and now I regret having adopted that stance. I refer to a Robert Frost poem 'Miles to go Before I Sleep.' I didn't release the pressure and always operated at high RPMs with quiet exhilaration.

Q – How many hours a week did you work?

A – Averaged 60.

Q – What one skill set has had the most significant impact on your success to date?

A – Empathy—some might see empathy as a weakness. I feel what others feel though and through impactful probing am able to discern and meet customer needs. Value is making customer's problems go away.

Q – What would you consider your biggest regret professionally?

A – I reference another movie 'Twenty Feet to Stardom,' about backup singers that bring harmony to the biggest bands in popular music. I never allowed myself to recognize or accept the fact that perhaps I was actually a very effective and successful Sales Professional.

Q – Talk about life/work balance and how you navigated that in your career?

A – Early in my career I lacked in that area due to my focus on goals and financial obligations that simply had to be met. I always took work home and after the kids were in bed I would reopen files and get back at it until late into the evening. Later on, I adopted a more sustainable approach where I booked time for family or made time to attend a child's play at school mid-afternoon. Sales Professionals work very long hours so taking a couple hours here and there to be at a special event is a great advantage for those in this career of selling.

Q – What key piece of advice would you offer to the person just starting their Professional Sales career?

A – Most Sales Professionals function in the 'why.' Come to grips as to why you will do what you want to do.

Q – What would the experienced, successful Tim say to the inexperienced Tim on day one of his career?

A – Let me tell you who you are. Allow me to be the voice of reason. You are fearfully and wonderfully made.

9

CODE OF ETHICS IN PROFESSIONAL SELLING

THIS CHAPTER IS paramount to the success of your career and to the reputation you will earn over the decades of your professional selling career. We already have discovered that people who earn their living selling stuff are often mistrusted. We also learned about the success triangle: KNOW, LIKE, & TRUST. If you become known as a person of unquestionable integrity, a man or woman of your word, you will succeed, providing you put in the work. Study and invest in yourself and never give up.

I adopted, then printed this list and carried it with me after earning my CSP designation. This code of ethics is thus copied, with permission from the Canadian Professional Sales Association:

1. Maintain honesty and integrity in all relationships with customers, prospective customers, and colleagues and continually work to earn their trust and respect.

2. Accurately represent my products or services to the best of my ability in a manner that places my customer and my company in a position that benefits both.

3. Respect and protect the proprietary and confidential information entrusted to me by my company and my customers and not engage in activities that may conflict with the best interests of customers or my company.

4. Continually upgrade my knowledge of my products, services, skills and my industry.

5. Use the time and resources available to me only for legitimate business purposes. I will only participate in activities that are ethical and legal and when in doubt, I will seek counsel.

6. Respect my competitors and their products and services by representing them in a manner which is honest, truthful and based on accurate information that has been substantiated.

7. Endeavor to engage in business and selling practices which contribute to a positive relationship with the community.

8. Assist and counsel my fellow Sales Professionals where possible in the performance of their duties.

9. Treat fellow members with special consideration, be part of a sales community, collaborate for coaching, guidance and information.

10. Abide by and encourage others to adhere to this member Code of Ethics.

10

GET A MENTOR THEN BE A MENTOR

THE FIRST RECORD of the word mentor is in 'Homer's Odyssey,' a favorite story in Greek mythology. When Odyssey was about to embark for the Trojan War, ultimately a 20 year journey, he left his son Telemachus with a friend named Mentor, a sage counsellor and advisor. Mentor served as the boy's tutor and guide.

Mentoring identifies a process in which a more experienced person assists a less experienced individual to grow and develop. Mentors might focus on a singular goal or on a broader set of goals and learning scenarios.

The person seeking a mentor is called the mentee. *If you are beginning your professional sales journey please seriously consider seeking out a mentor.* The person need not be a friend. I suggest you choose someone you may have been observing in your sector or company. They should be a person of high professional integrity, successful, and one whom you've noticed adheres to a code of ethics that aligns with your own ethics and values.

Most of us are aware of or familiar with unofficial mentoring. I have had several mentors in various arenas of life, but the mentorship was never made official. I considered them as my mentor, but they likely did not think of me as their mentee. It never occurred to me to ask someone to 'be my mentor,' considering I already perceived them to be a mentor to me. Looking back, I missed valuable opportunities to actually listen and learn vs. just quietly watching and learning.

As a young entrepreneurial professional seller you are going to ride the roller coaster of success and disappointment. You will deal with unscrupulous individuals, or perhaps work in a culture that could be too toxic for your liking. You might get fired once or twice, or have a season of what you feel is utter failure (as I did in my life insurance career). I didn't know where to turn, didn't know how to stop the quicksand from sucking me downward. I was lost, discouraged, and too embarrassed to ask for or find help. Looking back, had I sought out a mentor, I think I could have had a better chance of having succeeded in that industry.

Mentorships can be temporary or can change if the chemistry isn't evident. It is not an absolute necessity for there to be instant chemistry. In this relationship, it can be a friendship but is moreso a teacher / student relationship. You might not always like the homework or feedback, but as a mentee, you are being taught how to improve your skill set in your trade. There should be regular planned face-to-face communication at least once or twice monthly, plus some potential added email if necessary. At the front end you should agree this is a 12 month arrangement which provides for either party to leave the arrangement after the year is up. It is, of course, imperative that all conversations be held in strictest confidence.

The mentee should drive the relationship. You are the one asking for assistance, so it is you who sets up meetings and conversations. Your time should be limited to something each can adopt—30 or 45 minutes perhaps, but no longer. Share your goals, and barriers; maybe you are stuck and feeling discouraged after not hitting budget last month, or perhaps a large deal fell through. This is all normal activity in the life of a professional seller, and these are potential scenarios your mentor can help guide you through. When you find your perfect mentor, be certain to show sincere gratefulness for his or her investment into your life and career. *Your mentor is in a position to change your life.* When your life is ticking on all cylinders, your professional career has a far better chance of succeeding as well.

Don't assume you have to be old to be a mentor. You certainly won't be a selling mentor on day one but even today you can become a mentor to a young person. It is unlikely a 10 year old is going to walk up and ask you to be their mentor so keep your eyes open and look for an opportunity to touch a life.

If you are a mentor to someone already, congratulations! When you do become one be certain you *'connect before you correct.'* Take time to get to know your mentee and ask a plethora of questions to assess the temperament of the mentee in effort to determine what approach they will respond most positively to. You were likely pursued and asked to be their mentor. Consider it an honour to walk beside a mentee.

When I was 30, I made a commitment to become a Big Brother. I agreed, for one year, to provide friendship to a 5 year old boy from a father absent home. One year turned into two, five, ten, and fifteen, and I've now been his Big Brother for 36 years. My first and only little brother, Lonnie, is now 41 with a wife and two children. I was invited to be best man at his wedding, and have the honour of seeing him name his son Gregory.

Today, Lonnie (I call him Alvin) and I are great friends. Though he lives on the other side of Canada we find time to talk nearly every week. The mentorship started out as something I did for him but has resulted in multiple blessings for me and my family as well.

I read an interesting quote recently by Helen Walton who said "It's not what you gather, but what you scatter that tells what kind of life you have lived."

I encourage you to find a mentor and be one. Pay it forward!

BALKTALK #9 – Danger! Don't Miss That Step

It is important to recognize that when you miss a critical step in the selling process it can result in a failed effort.

In 2005 I had set a goal of earning my professional designation as a CSP (Certified Sales Professional). I studied for two years, putting off writing the exams, awaiting perfection in my studies and presentation skills. The designation required 80% pass rate in both a written exam and an oral presentation. Each exam occurred on a different date. I passed the written exam first. Then I prepared for my oral presentation portion. The exam was in Toronto so I drove there, the night prior. In my hotel room in front of the bathroom mirror, I created a presentation. I ensured I followed the steps of a great sales call, but needed something to practice with, so I looked around the room and grabbed a pen. I called it the Stealth pen and created a presentation. When I arrived for the exam I was set up in a small office, awaiting the examiner. I was not provided any information on the product I was 'selling' until that moment. Once the topic was provided I was given 5 minutes to prepare. The examiner set the scene. "Greg, you are at a trade show and have a booth, where your company sells promotional items, like golf balls, hats, shirts, small booklets and pens." He handed me a pen and said "your job is to convince me that my company should buy pens from you."

WHOA!!! Can you imagine? The very presentation I practiced for hours the night prior was exactly what I was to present. I smoothly and confidently presented my top grade Stealth pen. It was a spectacular and confident presentation (in my humble opinion). I had price points and discounts for volume purchases, I had different colours all with fine or medium points, and introduced different coloured ink and grips. I was given a very high grade, but I did not achieve the 'pass with honours' designation that I was aiming for. I had forgotten a key step in my presentation. I forgot to ask the examiner to <u>write with my pen</u>. I told him all about the quality ink and gold ballpoint, comfort grip and stainless steel pocket clip, and many other key features, but had forgotten to close with a test drive. Would you buy a car without driving it? No. You would not buy 1000 or more pens without writing with it either. I was horrified and disappointed, but once again we do learn our best lessons through failure. Though the exam was a mock sales call, I failed to execute in the fashion I should have.

Nevertheless, I earned my CSP designation and later took a number of other Management courses through the Canadian Professional Sales Association.

This inevitably proves a great plan with substandard execution can and will likely result in you seeing substandard results. Learn from my story. I did.

VOICE OF EXPERIENCE — Len Filiault —
Real Estate Sales Professional

Q – What age were you when you began your Professional Sales career?
A – I was 27.

Q – What were you selling at that point in your career?
A – I was a computer consultant at a retail outlet and was a Department Head. I then joined another computer business for a few years doing

corporate sales. I've been in the real estate industry for 6.5 years now, and I have now become a licensed Broker.

Q – How many years have you been in Professional Sales now?
A – 21 years.

Q – Looking back, how well prepared were you for the selling aspect of your career on day one?
A – Not at all. I had a factory job as a driver, delivering and picking up parts for customers. I do however, have strong technical skills which opened the door to sales.

Q – Talk about year one in the real estate business.
A – My first few months were pretty scary. I didn't know what I was doing and was questioning whether I had chosen the best career for me. I was beating myself up, was trying to advertise and scramble my way through it all. I knew I was in trouble so I looked within our organization for a rockstar realtor, and wanted to find a Christian to mentor me. I needed somebody to catch me doing things right and provide me some solid grounding in the business. Thankfully, I found a phenomenal mentor.

Q – Has discouragent been challenging at any point? If so, how did you journey through it?
A – Oh yes. I was very discouraged; however, *after 3 months of mentoring I was convinced that I could do the job and succeed.* I still wondered if I had the temperament for it, but was eventually invited to join a team of realtors where we work as a unit. It's been a truly wonderful experience. I have a great wife who allowed me to step out in faith to start this new career at 43 years old. Additionally, my wife's uncle played a key role in walking me through my early journey, offering me selling tips and encouraging me.

Q – What was/is the biggest challenge you face on a regular basis in selling?

A – Income inconsistency, since I no longer have that safe salary. I am 100% commissioned so I have wondered where my next listing is coming from and when. I am trying to trust in myself and build self-confidence. I feel awkward selling because real estate seems to be 90% selling of myself as a capable trustworthy professional and 10% selling the product.

Q – What has been the most substantial factor to any success you have experienced so far?

A – My faith. I literally have to trust God to direct my path and be my provider. I will not dilute my integrity to make a sale and God has honoured that commitment. Our entire team is made up of Christian business people and though the team concept is very uncommon in this sector, our team was #12 in the world in 2018 and #9 in 2019 in sales volume for Century 21.

Q – Has there been one key person who has consistently impacted your success journey? Why? Would you consider that person to be a mentor?

A – Absolutely! I now have several mentors, as each person on our team has become one. During those initial three months in the business, my key mentor kept pushing me and encouraging me to not quit. He was instrumental in seeing me through the rough patches.

Q – When you experience success do you allow yourself to bask in the sunshine?

A – Yes, I think so. I think 'we' do. Our team uses regular fund contributions to take fun trips with the spouses too which is pretty awesome. My wife and I saved up and put in a pool. I am not sure that I am emotionally basking yet. I am focused on how to keep building on whatever success does occur. My highlight listing has been a $2.4 million dollar home that sold in 3 months.

Q – How has COVID-19 altered or impacted your selling process?

A – During the first few weeks everyone was ultra cautious. I actually encouraged my clients not to list their homes for sale but to wait and see. We did, however, proceed to list vacant homes and show them, but it was too risky in my mind to be walking people through inhabited homes. Virtual tours had become popular prior to COVID-19, but had now become commonplace. Even during COVID-19 home sales have continued.

Q – How many hours do you work on average each week?

A – Likely 40-50, but it fluctuates in the real estate sector. COVID-19 reduced it to 25 sometimes, but in this business you work when there is work to be done. We were not doing any open houses so my weekends were a bit more free than normal.

Q – What one skill set has had the most significant impact on your selling career to date?

A – Honesty and integrity as per comments made by satisfied customers. I simply won't blow smoke to get a sale. Comments like that get around too.

Q – What would you consider to be your biggest regret to date?

A – I should have done far more homework regarding a real estate career and the industry in general. But hey, it's working out okay so far!

Q – Talk about work/life balance as a professional seller and how you navigate it.

A – I'm getting better at it now. My wife gave me five years to succeed in this business so I was really working long and hard. After two years it had become evident that my efforts were being blessed, and this is now my full-time forever career. I now have developed a far better balance for my wife and son.

Q – What key piece of advice would you offer to a young seller just starting their selling career?

A – Know yourself. Find a mentor. When ready, self invest and get your Broker's licence.

Q – What would the experienced Len tell the young Len on day one of your career?

A – Know and trust yourself. Have faith and confidence in yourself. Don't believe those who say only Type A personalities succeed in sales. Know your skill set and how to structure it to succeed. Treat each client with respect and understanding, and you'll have clients for life.

11

LISTENING SKILLS 101

MANY PEOPLE ASSUME that the best talkers make the most effective Sales Professionals. Yet in both my career and throughout life, I have noted that people are drawn to good listeners more than to smooth talkers. Everybody wants to be heard. As a Sales Professional you must develop the discipline of very effective listening skills. *There are five key levels of listening:*

Here but not hear:

Each and every one of us has had the experience of speaking to someone who we know isn't quite tuned into what we are saying. I can even sense this while on the phone. As a Sales Professional, you too might find yourself tuned out when your customers speak. Your mind might wander back to your previous sales call or your next call. Your eyes may glaze over, making it obvious to the client that you are absent at that moment. *You must stay emotionally present at each and every selling opportunity. Wandering minds miss important details. It's embarrassing to have to ask for something to be repeated or, worse yet, ask about something that was already shared.* The very worst is if you provide a solution that doesn't match the stated need. You have to be here, to hear.

Undigested words:

This occurs when you are tuned in well enough to hear the words spoken by the customer or speaker. Your brain has processed the fact you *know* what was said but you are so busy planning your next statement that you have not yet truly *digested* their comments. There might even be times when your current habit sees you interrupt the speaker to purge your thoughts before you forget them. ***Interrupting is a cardinal sin in professional selling.*** It tells your customer you don't value their comments as much as you do your own. Be certain you have heard and have digested before replying.

Calm absorption:

The speaker has completed their comments and you have allowed the words and meaning of the words to be absorbed. Take in the comments and digest them before planning your next step. Don't fear silence. It is not an indication of weakness. When you do speak, your spoken words will be derived from well-planned thoughts. ***Be aware of your own body language when listening.*** Folded arms indicate you disagree or do not want to engage in this particular conversation. Stay open to your customers' words, sit back, and show a relaxed willingness to absorb.

Empathetic recall:

Empathy is the ability to emotionally understand what other people feel. When you absorb a speaker's comments, especially when one on-one, send them a visual message that you value what they're saying. Our eyes tell stories, as does an occasional nod or a short "yes" or "uh huh," confirming your engagement. We have all had a conversation where the other person's eyes roll, or look away. Each action could indicate there is a potential problem or disagreement brewing. If you observe such, *stop and ask if what you've said makes sense. Make an effort to consider their comments and see the issue from their perspective.* It is always acceptable to ask for clarity if, at any point, you are not clear on what was stated or asked for. This is especially important if the customer wants you to find information on a topic or product. Be certain you understand his needs, and if not, circle back. Your customer will appreciate the opportunity to restate the need, and will see your level of interest and honesty.

Considerate response:

Have you heard the phrase "The customer is always right?" While the saying is well-known, the customer is often *not* right. However, when there is a differing opinion, it is critical to relationship growth to provide a non defensive, considerate reply. Your voice tone and inflexion will encourage further communication, providing each of you further opportunity to expand your thoughts. *Asking clarifying questions shows that you care about the customers' opinion, even though you might not agree.* If you fail at this step, you risk the customer shutting down the path of communication. If the communication ceases, no solution will be reached at all. This is especially evident with a phlegmatic personality who prefers peace. They might not actively say they disagree, but nor will they buy your product. Remember that you are selling to temperaments.

Summary

When your customers speak, try to envision a period at the end of their sentence before responding. It is perfectly acceptable to make notes while they are speaking if you ask for permission to do so. Ensure that you make one word notes so your eyes can quickly reconnect to the speaker, showing you are engaged in the conversation. When it is your turn to speak, you can refer to your notes and ask a meaningful, appropriate, open ended question.

Customers want to be heard, especially so when there is a situation of disappointment or dissatisfaction. Regardless of the product or service you sell, there will be a plethora of opportunities to prove that you are an effective problem solver. If your customer tells you his problem, ensure you have all the details concerning his complaint or concern. This is where you must make notes. Before you leave the call or hang up the phone, read back to him what you think you heard him say. This lets him know that you heard accurately and are well prepared to go away to seek the solution that addresses their specific need.

BALKTALK #10 – Ambiguity Kills—Clarity Wins

I've already highlighted that you ought not ever assume. The next aspect of integrity is to never present an ambiguous statement audibly or in writing. Be crystal clear on all aspects of the selling transaction. Provide clarity on the payment and credit terms of the agreement, warranty, service, return policy, and anything that impacts the customer's transaction satisfaction.

How often have you heard "read the small print"? How many radio ads have you heard where some guy speaks on super fast mode at the end of an advertisement whereby they can later state they told you the warranty was only 30 minutes but the speech was so sped up you couldn't decipher the words?

Whatever you sell, it is your professional responsibility to represent your products or services with honesty and integrity at all times regardless of the outcome. I made a commitment early in my career that I would never lie to win an order. I would never stretch the truth, state a delivery promise that was earlier than factual, and would be certain to address quality, warranty, and after-sale service. Whatever questions were asked of me I would answer with the truth as I knew it, otherwise would simply say I didn't know but would find out. As a new Sales Professional, you will garner a world of respect by telling the truth and delivering quality at every turn.

12

DEVELOP & COMMIT TO YOUR OWN CORE VALUES

OVER THE YEARS, I have heard the term core values at every seminar attended and it often caused deep thought and introspection. While each individual may use different words when asked to define 'core values', when unravelled, the meaning seems to be consistent. *Your core values are the belief system that ultimately dictates your behaviour in life's situations.* I imagine everyone would say they have a set of core values. Have you ever written them down and carried the list in your purse or wallet? You might have a set of personal and a set of professional core values or they might be the same list. *Failure to live by a quality set of core values will ultimately result in personal regret.*

As a Sales Professional, you get to make your own list. I cannot give you the list or suggest you adopt my list. You have the freedom to develop your own, and make your own deep commitment to live your life wrapped firmly around *your* value system. Your level of commitment will determine your level of success in all areas of life. Here are some key core values, many of which we've already touched on in previous chapters:

- Honesty – Speaking the truth even when it costs you something
- Integrity – Doing the right thing when you think nobody is watching
- Passion – The drive you feel in your heart for the activity pursued
- Empathy – Feeling the other party's emotions
- Perseverance – Grit and determination to keep going when the going gets tough
- Self Confidence – Strongly believing that you can do whatever you commit yourself to do
- Strong work ethic – Going beyond the call and DIRTFT—(do it right the first time)
- Competence – A commitment to being well versed on your topic or product
- Discipline – Doing the job well even when you don't feel like it
- Positive attitude – Imagining the best outcome in all situations
- Tenacity – Pursuing your goals with determination, focus and passion
- Reliability – Ensuring others can count on you to do what you said you'd do
- Consistency – Developing the habit of always following through on the task
- Courageousness – Driving through the fear
- Efficiency – Finding the most cost effective process while removing waste
- Accountability – Willingness to allow your process to be seen and accepting feedback
- Quality – Completing all tasks without shortcuts that impact negatively in any way

- Self respect – Adopting practises and disciplines that do no harm to yourself
- Mentorship – A willingness to seek experience and to pay your experience forward

I think you'll agree that each value has merit, yet *some are absolutely paramount to the long term success of a Sales Professional.* You might be able to add ten more based on your current core values and, if so, that is totally acceptable.

Congratulations for creating your list, writing it down, and carrying it with you from this day forward. Refer to it regularly, as well as when times get tough, or challenging decisions must be made.

BALKTALK #11 – Respect the Gatekeeper

Within the first week of your journey toward professional selling, you will likely encounter a Gatekeeper, depending on the sector you work in. This person's actual title will not be stated as such, but could be executive assistant, receptionist, or office manager. This individual is the first person you meet at your customer's place of business in the lobby or front office area. They are often the face of the company whose role is to welcome you but also to protect the building and staff from unwanted entrees. He or she will be well trained in how to deflect your attempts to gain critical contact names, phone numbers, or extension numbers. They certainly won't willingly pass along important cell numbers!

If you have an appointment, the Gatekeeper will have note of it and will allow you in. If you are making a cold call it could be a challenge to make any headway at all, especially if they are well trained. In my experience, they all know how to quickly send you on your way.

Typically, though, when you have an appointment you will be asked to wait a few minutes while your customer prepares for your visit. Recall that you have seven seconds to make a good first impression. During the wait, seek an opportunity to chat briefly with the Gatekeeper. They often have a myriad of responsibilities and perhaps a large switchboard to manage so be respectful of their tasks. Be open and friendly. You can choose to discuss the weather, traffic patterns today, ask him or her how the day has been, or make a sincere comment on the beauty of the building or landscaping. Find a way to take them off the defensive. One of my major customers had a waterfall wall behind the Gatekeeper's desk. This provided an immediate opportunity to compliment that feature. She was quick to talk about how it was designed and built. Over the next ten years she was increasingly open as I arrived for my appointments, but it all began with a simple compliment.

Gatekeepers know just about everything that goes on at their workplace. Through my friendly interactions with hundreds of Gatekeepers, I have found that you can often gain insights that even your own contacts won't share. They know what new contracts have been awarded, how many people work there, who their largest customers are, what expansions are potentially planned, and can often be an avenue for discovering new contacts if you ask in an appropriate fashion, after developing some rapport.

Don't abuse the privilege of this relationship. If anyone in management thinks you have stepped off- side regarding your line of questioning it can harm the overall relationship.

The Gatekeeper is a goldmine of information. Handle with care.

13

VOICES FROM THE INTERIOR

WE ALL HAVE heard the voices our brain sends us. Perhaps they are positive messages: You have a four foot putt on the 18th hole to beat your partner and win a hotdog and a beverage. You hear the voice that says "you got this Greg—straight back and through—easy putt." Or perhaps on the 17th you just missed a three foot putt and now the voice says "you likely won't make the putt, so get ready to pull out your wallet Greg." Which voice am I going to listen to?

I strongly believe that ***what you say is what you get. If you say you will succeed as a Sales Professional you will.*** If you tell yourself you will likely fail, then you will. Whether you think you can succeed or you tell yourself you won't, you will be correct. You must be fearless to walk this journey. Tara Sloan from Hockey Night in Canada states that being fearless doesn't mean you don't have fear. It means that despite the fear you persevere through it. One of my Voice of Experience guests, Tim spoke transparently about his fear and how he endured through it with grit and perseverance.

I have often noticed a pro golfer with his eyes closed just before attempting an important putt. He is creating a vision of the ball going into the hole. The putt could be worth $1.2 million though, not a hotdog. As a Sales Professional you also must envision success. You must see yourself making that important presentation, envision people nodding as you make critical points and embracing what it is you are delivering. You see the customer loving the house you will show them this afternoon or the young couple signing for that new vehicle. How you think is portrayed in how you speak, and how your body language sends messages to your buyers.

As a Junior Sales Professional it can take time to develop the vision of success. Remember the interview with Len? Recall how the voice was asking him to doubt his decision to remain in the real estate business? Soon thereafter, though, he had the wisdom to seek out a mentor, who quickly replaced the internal voice with an audible one, encouraging Len to hang in there. He also started to catch Len doing things right. A new voice started to take over inside Len's brain and heart. A passion was brewing and a refreshed confidence was stirring. Len crossed the decision bridge when he said "I can do this." Such an awesome realization. You, too, will stand on this very bridge. Will you cross it or retreat? I say you'll cross and succeed.

It is normal to have to persevere through the times when your confidence takes a hit and you doubt your abilities. Just remember that if the mountain were smooth, you couldn't climb it. ***Those voices will be present your entire career: but how you manage the voices will determine your destiny.*** The more times you allow yourself to celebrate those small victories, the larger your memory library grows. You will recall a similar situation where you succeeded. You'll recall how you sold to this customer's temperament last time. You need to become proficient at self talk. Rinse the negative. You will not succeed at 100% of your efforts, so realistically manage your expectations. Recall the baseball greats that failed 70% of the time? If a baseball player thinks he will strike out, chances are he will be correct 100% of the time.

In the early months of your selling career, your memory bank is going to be empty until you make some successful deposits. I vividly recall, as a very young boy opening my first bank account at the CIBC in Essex, ON. Mom took me in and I was treated like an adult. We sat on nice chairs and I had $3.00 to deposit. I still have that bank book today. I recall asking where my money was going to be kept, and then asking why I would not be given back the same actual dollar bills that I had deposited. The teller was very kind and considerate and Mom explained it again that evening. Then I made future deposits. You will start making memory deposits immediately, however until you actually perform the job of selling, you won't have deposited much into your success bank. But over the next year your deposits will be many.

Over that first year or two or five or twenty five, what voices might you hear? I can tell you that even after 4 decades there were times when I still heard voices, and had to persevere through fear or intimidation. About a year prior to retiring I was asked to do a presentation at our company AGM. The regional general manager asked me to speak and gave me no parameters. He said "I trust you". That was huge, but crafting a 20 minute presentation in front of all my peers and upper management was scary. Following the presentation I was provided some exceedingly positive feedback from many of my peers, but one manager in particular, Bryan Sidhu, who has been in the business for many years said it was the best presentation on selling he had ever heard. His opinion mattered to me. The many compliments from my peers impacted dramatically on me.

So what voices might you hear and have to fight off? Recall when I was told I was too young to succeed in sales? I heard that voice loudly for a period of time. You might hear that the customer likely won't grant you the appointment, or when you get there he will not keep the appointment. You will hear that you aren't skilled enough, don't have your degree in business, or you won't be liked and thus will never build your success triangle. The voice might tell you that your purchase order will be given to their previous preferred source. It might whisper that they likely won't want to buy the house you are showing them, or the financing likely won't be approved for that $50,000 truck. You must learn to manage the negative voices or they will manage you. *Repeat—you must learn to manage the negative voices or they will manage you.*

Whether you're a newer Sales Professional or you're more experienced, realize that words have power, but only as much power as you grant. If you plant negative seeds, expect a negative crop. If you want success, surround yourself with positive, successful people. Engage with those who will hold you up when you stumble or get discouraged. Speak words of success to yourself. Find the group that succeeds and hang around that positive energy. You will recall that is exactly what Len did. He sought out a rockstar realtor in his office and asked that person to mentor him.

Joel Osteen has a book called 2 Words That Will Change Your Life Today. The two words are I AM. You can tell yourself that you are too young, too short, too uneducated, too shy, not blessed with the ideal temperament for selling, too old to start a professional sales career, not networked well enough, not popular, not able to learn the product, not smart enough to pass the licensing exam, not good looking enough, not articulate enough, and so on.

You must rinse that negative self talk and start saying "I AM exactly the right age to begin my Professional Sales career, I AM going to find the perfect mentor, I AM smart, I AM popular, I AM confident, I AM going to be well liked by customers, I AM qualified and creative, I AM resilient, I AM a great closer, I AM going to develop the skill set needed for selling, I AM going to be financially rewarded, I AM successful, talented, positive, happy, energetic, focused and disciplined. I AM honest and filled with integrity. I AM going to develop a great list of core values and live by them. I AM going to do this! I AM going to become a successful Sales Professional!

I have experienced many peaks and valleys in my selling career but often heard my father's words: I heard him tell somebody else one day that "Greg could sell hot water bottles in the desert." He wasn't aware I heard him say that phrase, but those words were powerful. What if I had heard him say "Greg couldn't sell ice in the desert?" Would I have given up? Words can be medicine or poison. ***Words have the power to transform lives.***

Start each day by telling yourself who you want to be. You might not have all the attributes you wish on day one of your career, but keep telling yourself you do. You'll speak truth into your future success. I bet you've heard the popular phrase "fake it til you make it." Words are powerful. Use with caution. You cannot unring a bell. Harmful, hurtful words ring loudly forever. Start now catching others doing things right and tell them so, but just as importantly, ***catch YOURSELF doing things right*** and be encouraged. Rinse and repeat.

In the past, I have heard many negative voices in my own head, yet I succeeded by choosing to listen to a different voice. A few years ago I had an MRI examination. During a phone interview prior to the MRI, I was asked if I had ever had one and asked if I was claustrophobic. I said I had had an MRI before and was not claustrophobic. The exam was scheduled for 10:30 pm. When I arrived I was given the same questionnaire I had completed by phone the previous day. I told the nurse, and she smiled and said it was protocol to do it again to be certain the answers were consistent. Next, I was gowned up and went into the room where the MRI machine was. Again, I did the interview for the third time. However this time, when I saw the machine, I realized I had never had an MRI but a CT scan. The nurse explained that I would lie on a long narrow board which appeared half the necessary width (based on my width), and be transferred into an area that appeared to be the size of a furnace heat duct. She told me I'd be given a headset and asked me what kind of music I liked. I was also given a panic button in case I wanted out. Why would I want out? The MRI exam would only take 17 minutes. The nurse proceeded to move me into this extremely tight area. Music never played, and the slamming of the magnets began. I made the mistake of opening my eyes. There was a light about a half inch from my face and I was jammed into an extremely small space. Now I began to sweat, and water was literally pouring off my forehead. My heart was literally audible in my headset pounding like never before. I assume I was having a panic attack though I had never experienced one prior. A great friend, who was a doctor, had arranged this immediate MRI as a favour to me, as it often took six months to get an MRI. As I laid there, a voice in my head asked, "What if you have a heart attack in here and die? Would anyone know for 17 minutes?" The panic button was in my left hand but I dare not wimp out and push it. After all, hundreds of other people were waiting six months for their MRI, and Doctor Smith had arranged this for me in one day. I had to suck it up. I quickly started a deep breathing technique and talked myself into believing I would not die in there. The new messages in my head were "What a stupid thing to think Greg. This is just a test and surely you can lay still for another 16 minutes." The self talk went on until the magnets stopped. My gown was sopping wet and I wondered if water had escaped from any other body orifice. The nurse asked "How was that?" but could see I was soaked. I said "well, that was a bit weird," not really sharing my utter frightful experience. Following the MRI, I read a book called Change your Brain—Change your Life. A year later I needed another MRI, only this time I completed the multiple questionnaires, claimed no claustrophobia and completed the MRI easily and dry as a bone. I adopted new thinking, invited new voices, and almost fell asleep during the magnetic pounding. I had changed my brain. You can too! No negative voices allowed!

Throughout the current pandemic, the top doctor in British Columbia, Dr. Bonnie Henry did a daily televised COVID-19 update and always ended her presentation with these words: "Be kind, be calm, be safe." We should live by those words!

Recommended reading: Change your Brain—Change Your Life by Dr. Daniel Amen

---

BALKTALK #12 – Be Good to Yourself—You Matter!

You have 8,760 hours over 52 weeks every year. We should all ensure that we get at least 8 hours of restful sleep each night, meaning we sleep 2,920 hours each year. We then are awake for 5,840 hours. How should you use and invest that time for maximum health, effectiveness, and happiness?

Many people have four weeks of vacation plus ten personal days throughout the year for Christmas, Easter, and other special days our government allows for. Lets state that in a typical year, you will work 46 weeks and if you work 50 hours a week, you're working for 2,300 hours. You now have 3,540 hours to do whatever you want to do. This equates to 26% of your 8,760 waking hours working, 33% sleeping, leaving 41% for what we shall call leisure time. Wow, it sure doesn't seem like we have 41% of our time to do whatever we want, does it? The good news is that for those who work less the leisure hours increase.

Our leisure hours are often heavily tasked with chores, meals, laundry, housekeeping and repairs, outdoor yard work, shopping, running kids to school and sporting events, church activities, visiting friends, and then the all-important TV and social media time. Is it any wonder we feel exhausted and overwhelmed?

Let me stop the presses and say this: "ALWAYS take your vacation time." I have known Sales Professionals who get 4-6 weeks vacation and don't take time off. They then wonder why they are never refreshed, why their emotional tank is dry, and exhaustion has taken over. They get cranky and potentially risk their health all for the excuse (not reason) that they are too busy to take their family on a well-deserved vacation. Your family sees how hard you work each week and they, too, probably think you deserve a break. It is mutually beneficial to go away on an annual vacation. We have over 100 photo albums of family vacations, and though our daughters are now in their 30's they can often be found on our couch looking at those albums. They often laugh at the haircuts or matching outfits, but have vivid memories of time together as a family. Reward yourself, reward your family, and reward your employer. Your refreshed body and mind will pay mutual dividends.

Let's not skirt the issue of stress. Professional selling is not what many think it is or what you may have assumed. We truly don't plot all the Starbucks and golf courses and hang out there on a daily basis. Your company is going to expect you to exceed sales budgets, profit targets, and unit sales, and as the vice gets turned, you will feel the heat. It is imperative you research strategies on how to effectively handle stress and be open to asking for help when you feel it negatively impacts your wellbeing. Unaddressed stress can result in depression, heart disease, and other health ailments. It is not recommended that you 'suck it up' and ignore it. There is far more assistance today around mental health than ever before and many companies have an Employee Assistance Program, a 100% confidential provision of help in many areas. One of those is stress management. Use it when you need it. Then take a vacation.

VOICE OF EXPERIENCE — Evan Goode — Real Estate Sales Professional

Q – What age were you when you began your professional sales career?

A – I was 20.

Q – What were you selling at that point in your career?

A – For a short period I was in multi-level marketing, then sold advertising for the phone book. It was 100% commission based, and a huge challenge to sell $4000.00+ ads, since the company I was with was somewhat new and was not as well recognized as our competitors. Next, I held a selling role at Bell selling retail phones and telecom services, then onto Shaw Communications in an inside sales role where much of my selling was by phone and the income was quite good. I knew I could successfully sell by now.

Q – How many years have you been a full time Sales Professional?

A – Well let's refer to that as my real estate career which is 8 years.

Q – Looking back, how well prepared were you for the selling aspect of your career on day one?

A – Quite well prepared by the time I began my real estate career, as I received excellent sales training during my former jobs.

Q – Talk about year one in selling.

A – I did a lot of cold calling and learned how to assess and sell to different temperaments. I had a really good sales trainer, and I self-invested by diving into many books on selling techniques.

Q – Has discouragement ever been a challenge? If so, how did you journey through it?

A – Definitely—yes for sure. My first job was the most discouraging: full commission and no financial safety net at all. I could literally work all day and make zero dollars. I became heavily invested in myself, reading positive and uplifting books, one of which was Secrets of the Million Dollar Mind. I read dozens of books to keep myself motivated.

Q – What was/is the biggest challenge you face on a regular basis in selling?

A – Dealing with highly emotional people. I guess I prefer logical customers.

Q – What has been the most substantial factor contributing to any success you've experienced?

A – Most definitely creating strong work habits and routines. Each day I prime myself, get up early, read uplifting books, meditate, feed myself positive content, and ensure I am not reactionary when the work day starts. I am well prepared.

Q – Has there been one key person who has consistently impacted on your success journey? Would you consider that person to be your mentor?

A – Yes I have had a couple mentors really. Early on, I found a mentor in that multi level marketing role I spoke of. He was very motivational. Over the past seven years my broker and owner of the company, A.J. Hazzi has been my investment mentor, and has supported my efforts all the way.

Q – When you experience a successful chapter in your journey do you allow yourself to bask in the sunshine?

A – Yes, but I don't spend a lot of time celebrating. I would like to celebrate the wins somewhat better. At times I have set really big goals and when achieved, I often feel a bit low. I've learned that I need to be setting many goals, so when one is achieved I can celebrate that one while immediately moving toward the next and simultaneously have many on the go. I have found that expectations can leave me a bit disappointed at times too. I need to maintain realistic expectations.

Q – How has COVID-19 altered your selling process and what impact has it had on your success?

A – The first couple weeks things slowed right down and I started to plan what I would do during the pandemic: what hobbies might I engage in or what new language could I learn to speak. But within a few weeks business seemed to start up again and I've been as busy as ever starting in April. Then May, June and beyond were great. Some processes have changed. We don't share vehicles and there are no open houses. We are seeing more virtual tours and trying to more accurately assess how serious a buyer is before actually showing the property in person. There has certainly been more home office time, too, but with a one year old baby it has been great to spend time with him.

Q – How many hours do you work each week on average?

A – In this business it can change from 35 to 60 easily. It all depends on the market conditions and listings, client interest, etc. Lots of priming going on.

Q – What one skill set has had the most significant impact on your success to date?

A – My ability to activate good probing skills in effort to determine customer needs and find a solution that suits them. I also have a high energy level and lots of self motivation.

Q – What would you regard as your most significant professional regret to date?

A – No regret really. Each sales role I have had has contributed and impacted my current success journey.

Q – Talk about any work/life balance challenges and how you navigate that?

A – In real estate it is hard to shut off the brain. I am disciplining myself to set time aside and literally shut it off now. It is a challenge when working right here in town but when I am on vacation outside the city I delegate work to other team members and the work gets done effectively. I don't work on Sundays and often take one month's vacation to rest and recharge. Have been to Bali, Vietnam, Spain and Thailand for 3-4 weeks at a time.

Q – What key piece of advice would you offer a person just beginning their career as a Sales Professional?

A – Whatever selling experience you have had, learn from it; especially if you truly want this career. Be certain you have a passion for selling. Learn from every failure. Invest in self development and set really big goals for yourself.

Q – What would the experienced Evan tell the young Evan on day one of his career?

A – Invest in real estate as early as you can. I started my career in real estate relatively young but all my sales jobs taught me valuable lessons which now contribute to my success.

14

THE SALES PROFESSIONAL 'TOTAL PACKAGE'

THROUGHOUT THIS BOOK you've repeatedly read the term Sales Professional. Having been in the selling sector for four decades, I have certainly observed many professional sellers but have also seen some mere sales people. There is a definite difference! You must create your reputation as a Sales Professional in an effort to be respected and to succeed. What are some actions you can take to transform from salesperson to Sales Professional? In this chapter I touch on many topics that contribute to creating and ensuring you become the total package.

Because you are assessed by others within 7 seconds, it is imperative that you dress for success. Appearance matters. You don't have to wear a tuxedo or evening gown but you should look the part and dress appropriately for your selling sector. The term 'business casual' was born many years ago, which meant that my suits, sport jackets, and ties are used far less often. Weddings and funerals have been the key reasons I dig out the good stuff.

When I was a young boy, I recall telling my Mom that when I grew up I wanted a job where I could dress nice and get lots of mail. I must have thought those two elements meant one was important. Who knew that one day I would be receiving 150 emails daily? As it turns out, you can dress well without a suit or tie and look awesome and professional. Female Sales Professionals should be certain to dress conservatively professional. Dress pants and dresses are certainly acceptable, but be aware of your skirt length and blouse style. Whether male or female, how you dress and how you present yourself says a lot about who you are or at least how you will be perceived.

When I was a regional sales manager, I picked up one of the sellers to make some coaching calls together. He got into my vehicle and appeared he had washed his shirt, rolled it into a ball, let it dry for three days and put it on. I asked if he owned an iron to which he looked totally stunned and said he did. I urged him to return to his house and either find a pressed shirt or iron the one he had on. We were going nowhere looking like that. The rest of the day went exceedingly well.

Grooming is another aspect other people will judge. My daughters state that women with longer hair have an advantage here, as they can pull hair back into a ponytail, put on some mascara, and go quickly if they must. Adopting a modern hair style is a great contribution to overall appearance. Men should be certain to get a haircut when needed. If you have a beard, moustache, or goatee, keep it trimmed in a professional fashion. Always check your beard for food after each meal. It is horribly distracting to be speaking to someone with lunch in their beard.

Some people sweat more than others. For men, wearing a tee shirt under your dress shirt helps with underarm water rings so wear one. If you prefer an open collar, I suggest a v-neck tee shirt.

Hygeine is important! Always be showered and clean prior to all sales calls. You won't be invited back if your body odour creates a cloud in the room. Many companies have adopted a scent free work environment, so leave your cologne and perfume at home.

Bad breath is also a sale killer. I once made calls with a smoker but before each customer we saw that day he reached under his car seat, pulled out mouthwash and rinsed. Gum and breath mints work wonders, but get rid of both before speaking to the customer.

Does grammar matter? As a Sales Professional you will utilize a myriad of communication tools. You'll be using your cell phone to text, send email, using Facebook, Instagram, Twitter or LinkedIn and of course face-to-face or virtual meetings via Zoom or other means. Using proper grammar in print is essential, as it creates a perception of how intelligent you are. There are a myriad of homonyms, homophones, and homographs you need to be aware of and use properly in effort to be perceived as someone who has a firm grasp on the language you speak. The most glaring challenge seems to be the homophones. It is critical that you become adept in the utilization of words such as there / their / they're, to / too, our / hour, or cell / sell, its / it's, and ad /add.

There are many more but the two that many struggle with are there / their / they're and to / too. Everyones knows that two is the measure of quantity.

Let's look at examples on how to apply each.

There: I'm about to go over **there** on Friday to see my customer. **There** will be lunch served.

Their: I went to see my customer but **their** office closed early today.

They're: My customer's office closed early today but **they're** reopening tomorrow. This is the short form for the phrase **they are = they're.**

To: I went **to** pick up the purchase order this morning.
Too: There were **too** many people in line at the bank today, so I used the drive through.

Finally, please learn how to correctly use the words saw and seen. Once again, this will create a negative perception of you, if used incorrectly. There is a tendency to say "I seen it" whereas the correct version is "I saw it." When using the word seen, it is typically preceded with words like were, have, has or had. For instance, I have seen the customer at the trade show today. I saw him arrive around 9:00 a.m. Saw is the past tense of the verb see. Seen is the past participle of the verb see.

Over time your ability to effectively express your thoughts will improve, if you work at it. Having the ability to articulate your thoughts and ideas fluidly, without the um and uh sentence fillers will truly impact your presentations in a positive fashion. Avoid using 'like' as another filler when speaking your thoughts. As an example–"ok so like I went to the customer's office and he, like was late arriving so like, I waited for 30 minutes and then had to leave."

I love listening to professional speakers and presenters who can move through their presentation without utilizing any 'um, uh or like' in their sentences. Joel Osteen is one of the best. Past President Barack Obama is an astute speaker as well.

In my regional sales manager role, I was making coaching calls with my most senior Sales Professional. He was a true professional in every way. He was well respected, technically astute, always well dressed with shirts firmly pressed, and his shoes polished. He had many loyal customers who respected him. He did, however, struggle to communicate his thoughts without enormous use of um and uh. I once counted 103 times he used the fillers in one sales call. He wasn't even aware of his habit and did work on improving it. In his case, I cannot know whether it negatively impacted his selling results, because he always excelled, but as he became aware and started actually hearing himself saying um or uh, his presentation skills improved dramatically.

Eventually as a Sales Professional you will speak to more than one person / customer at a time. Perhaps one day you will speak to a room full of people. Developing good presentation skills is a critical element to succeeding. You will want to become astute at using Powerpoint, of course, but learning to speak comfortably in public is essential. Toastmasters International is an organization that operates clubs for the purpose of promoting communication, public speaking, and leadership. There is probably a Toastmasters International in your city. This is an ideal way to meet others on the same journey you are on, and do so in a comfortable, non intimidating fashion in effort to accomplish your goals and achieve personal and professional growth.

As a Sales Professional, there will come a day when you will need to address the awkwardness of a bribe. Maintaining the relationship, while professionally deflecting the bribe, ensures your customer isn't offended or embarrassed but also sends them a clear message that you will not erode your level of professionalism in exchange for their business. How will you recognize a bribe? It occurs when the customer makes it obvious there is an expected gift or some form of remuneration prior to the award of business. It could come in a very overt fashion or somewhat shaded in verbage you are expected to pick up on. In my career it occurred when a buyer at a huge corporation made it abundantly clear he wanted a new refrigerator and stove in exchange for a large contract we were negotiating for. There have been other less extravagant hints presented to those under my guidance as well. This is where your core values kick in, and your code of ethics take precedence. It is critical to maintain professional conduct and any conversation surrounding the topic should be friendly but direct with regard to the fact it is illegal and can be met with being fired. All requests should be reported to your superior.

Is a gift the same as a bribe? No it isn't but the larger valued the gift is, the more it can be construed as a bribe. As a Sales Professional you will know in your gut why you have provided the gift and so will your customer. Many companies hand out hats, shirts, jackets or pens, writing pads and golf balls all with their logo imprinted. These are items categorized under the heading of advertising expenses and can be given away without question. A new set of golf clubs—not so much. I truly believe some common sense will keep you out of hot water but again if in question speak to your superior before engaging in any questionable practise. If in doubt—DON'T!

Attitude determines altitude. As you journey through your career you might notice that it isn't always those with the most professional degrees, from the most prestigious schools, who hold the highest positions. You'll often find those with sharpened skills and heightened people skills are in leadership positions. As a Sales Professional it is imperative that you maintain a great attitude in the storm. There will be storms. There will be valid reasons to get sour over things that occur, or over decisions made that seem to hinder your process. Don't give in to a negative or toxic culture that might be evident in the very organization you are working for. All companies are made up of human beings, not all of whom will think like you do. I will admit to times when I got sucked into the vortex of participating in complaining. Be the person who brings a consistently great attitude to the workplace and watch your altitude rise above the storm.

Sales Professionals invest in themselves. I strongly suggest you engage in self improvement by earning your CSP designation or one equal to it. The Canadian Professional Sales Association (CPSA) is a spectacular option if you live in Canada. You might also investigate The Association of Professional Sales. Additionally there is a new professional sales designation being launched in early 2021. The Institute for Professional Advancement (IPA) is introducing the designation identified as the Certified Professional Sales Consultant (CPSC). Please investigate what is available in your geographical area. The CPSA statistics, measured over a 20 year period depict that 72% of those who graduate with their CSP designation rank in the top 25% of sales in their organization. The stats also indicate that 50% of the graduates earned more money after completing the course. A continuous improvement trajectory is essential to complete the total Sales Professional package.

If you want to enjoy something, proceed to participate in it occasionally with little regard to results. If you want to get good at something you will need to engage in it more often and discipline yourself to practice. If you want to be great at anything you must commit yourself to a continuous improvement trajectory, by seeking a coach and mentor. You must practice your trade daily. You will need to invest in yourself through continuous learning or education, reading and studying and by doing. Having a love and passion for selling will impact on your 'never give up' attitude toward becoming a great Sales Professional.

As a Sales Professional you will sell to every nationality or group imaginable. It is never acceptable to make comments of a discriminatory nature in front of or behind the backs of anyone. Ensure you never participate in another person's attempt to draw you into such a conversation either. You must stand up for what is right, proper, and ethical in all situations. Adopt this now and you'll never slip up and cost you the priceless respect of your colleagues or customers.

BALKTALK # 13 – Booze and Bad Language

Another form of professional conduct needs to be addressed now. Eventually you will be in the presence of your suppliers, competitors, and industry leaders. Many business sectors hold golf tournaments, curling bonspiels, regular industry association meetings, Rotary, Kinsmen, Lion's Club, company awards banquets, AGM, Christmas parties, and other social events. Your 'professional conduct' is another means by which you will be assessed, perceived, and respected as a professional. I have seen way too many inebriated colleagues embarrassing themselves and the company they represent at various functions.

Many years ago, a seller from a competitor was charged with a DUI and lost his license for one year. Since he was the company's key seller he was faced with either being fired or hiring a chauffeur at his own cost for a year in effort to keep his job. He chose the chauffeur route but his reputation certainly took a hit. I also recommend not consuming alcohol at lunch time. Your customers do not want the smell of beer or booze on your breath during your afternoon selling opportunities.

Remember—'you are always on stage.' Someone is watching.

What about vulgar language, off colour jokes, and swearing? I have heard some say that it is ok to adopt the language of the customer. Personally I think that's bunk! Developing the ability to professionally articulate your thoughts either in regular normal conversation or in formal presentations is imperative to earning and retaining a professional reputation. I once worked with a man for almost ten years when I heard him say to someone else "geez I have worked with Balkwill for ten years and never even heard him say damn." It is likely good he didn't hear my thoughts at times.

Early in my career I made a decision to communicate as best and clearly as possible without the use of off colour language and it has served me well. Not one customer ever refused to buy because I didn't swear and not many made mention of the fact I didn't. One thing you do risk by using vulgar language is that your customer doesn't, and won't buy from someone who does. Professionals don't need to fill their sentences with four letter words—okay, I think we can make an exception for 'SOLD'.

15

NETWORKING AND SOCIAL MEDIA

WOW, HOW TIMES have changed. I wasn't around to feed dinosaurs but four decades ago, believe it or not, nearly nobody had a cell phone. I do recall my brother-in-law getting one the size of a shoe box. He paid $1,500 for it. I admit he looked pretty cool holding a phone to his ear while driving down the highway, which was not illegal at the time? Today, the Sales Professional needs to accept the fact that he is not only on stage, but could also be on camera. Everyone has a cell phone now. The Police Associations around the globe have certainly realized that in the past few months. I doubt that many of us are on camera many minutes a day, but rest assured your customers may have many cameras. Some are located in their lobby, offices, hallways, and manufacturing areas. Once again, your conduct must be unquestionable.

The act of networking is as old as the hills. There have always been clubs and associations where like-minded people gather, discuss topics of mutual interest, and share stories. I once was a member of the Windsor Executives Association. Each week, members met at a very nice restaurant and shared information on how we could mutually benefit from doing business with one another. There was a measure of accountability as well, since each week we'd go around the room stating who we had supported that week, given business to, received business from, or sent a lead their way. It was a fantastic and impactful group of professionals.

Over the years I have taken opportunities to network, whether on a church board, a strata board, volunteering opportunities or within other industry related organizations. Being in leadership positions for much of my professional life has opened doors to meet other professionals in positions of leadership, and observe different communication and leadership styles. Many of my friends have been business owners or executives in their sectors which provided me important insight to many types of businesses I would otherwise not have known much about.

As a Sales Professional you will have access to many communication platforms. Social media provides a myriad of opportunities to showcase homes, automobiles, boats, RVs, or other products you might represent. Sales Professionals need to recognize the risks you take when posting opinions on issues that impact the globe. Your political opinion could impact a sale or, more importantly, a relationship. Do your customers need to know what you think of the leader of another country? You only get a vote in your country. There has been a lot of troubling footage on the news relating to racism and policing this year. It is imperative to remain kind and considerate while posting on social media. Messenger provides a more confidential mode of communciation, but it can still impact future business should your opinions lack respect or are insensitive. You are risking your own level of perceived professionalism by posting on issues of conflict. You do so at your own risk.

On the positive side, social media gives you an opportunity to showcase your professionalism, draw customers to your website based on your posts, and grow your business by staying professional and respecting a code of conduct, while also respecting others.

In all my professional life I have never seen someone as effective at networking than my next Voice of Experience guest. He drips of professionalism and is a man of high integrity.

VOICE OF EXPERIENCE — Mark Morris — Security Systems Sales Professional

Q – What age were you when you began your professional sales career?
A – 25.

Q – What were you selling at that point in your career?
A – I worked at a pharmaceutical plant and realized it wasn't the career I really wanted. An opportunity came to join a local company selling electronic voice pagers. The pagers let users receive an urgent or important message from someone, since cell phones were not popular yet. Realtors could get a 'page' alerting them to call the office or call home. Doctors could be alerted if their patient was about to deliver a baby. It was new and exciting.

Q – How many years have you been a full-time Sales Professional?
A – 35.

Q – Looking back, how well prepared were you for the selling aspect of your career on day one?
A – Well I wasn't afraid at all. I have great social skills, am an effective problem solver, and while selling pagers, learned a lot about the sales process. The transition felt seamless.

Q – Talk about your first year as a Sales Professional.

A – I loved selling. I was selling beepers and pagers and the product was about 2" square and was being well received.

Q – Has discourgamenet ever been challenging at any point? If so how did you journey through it?

A – No—not often, fortunately. I was originally selling beepers and cell phone technology but the last 20 years have been selling security systems and technology. I make people see that I want to be their friend and take away their problem. Losing business based on price has at times been discouraging but I always move on quickly. There are more sales to pursue.

Q – What was/is your biggest challenge you face on a regular basis in sales?

A – Fortunately I have primarily sold products that suit all types of customers. I have accumulated a large wealth of customers and contacts. Today, meeting the immediate response of the expectations of customers can at times be challenging. Life is moving fast for all of us.

Q – What has been the most substantial factor to any success you have experienced?

A – Persistence. I hang on and stay in touch until the customer says no thanks and is firm in his answer. I do seek to find what the barrier was regarding the lost sale. Following up on every quote is critical.

Q – Has there been one key person who has consistently impacted on your success journey to date? If so, would you consider that person to be a mentor?

A – Not really. But there are a couple men that have been helpful at points in my career.

Q – When you experience a successful chapter in your journey do you allow yourself to bask in the sunshine?

A – Yes I do. I keep an especially close eye at month end. Even during COVID-19 I hit my monthly targets. To celebrate a win I will sometimes take a 3 day weekend to reflect, recharge, and take a breath.

Q – How has COVID-19 altered your selling process and what impact has it had on your success?

A – There has been much more pressure to hit my goals and thus would say I have put in 10-15% more work, which has included working some weekends. My actual process has not changed though.

Q – How many hours per week do you work on average?

A – 45-50 on average.

Q – What one skill set has had the most significant impact on your success to date?

A – Honesty and integrity. I absolutely will not lie to make a sale. If I absolutely cannot meet their needs and I know my competitor has a better solution, I will send him there. Earning their trust is critical and maybe next time he'll return to me, knowing I will only sell him the right solution.

Q – What would you regard as your most significant regret professionally?

A – Twice I actually resigned and left the company I work for today and though it is strictly against company policy to take back those who resign they took me back both times. In all I have been here 35 years and grateful to be here.

Q – Talk about work/life balance and how you navigate that.

A – There is a family joke that I really only work part time. As a Sales Professional there are times when I might play golf on a Friday or run an errand for my family or grandkids. In exchange, I will work Saturday though. We truly have flex schedules when in a selling profession.

Q – What key piece of advice would you offer to the person who is just beginning their career as a Sales Professional?

A – Become proficient at networking with business groups, whether breakfast clubs, or those similar to Windsor Executives, sector associations, etc. It is especially important for a new Sales Professional to get connected quickly.

Q – What would the experienced Mark tell the young Mark on his first day in your career?

A – I would encourage and challenge him to always be persistent. Make the commitment to do what needs to be done to realize success. Get plugged in. Also know when to say no. Sometimes what a customer wants and how they want it can rub me the wrong way. Know when to fire a customer. In the end, certain high maintenance customers turn out to be just that.

16

INTERNAL CUSTOMERS ARE CRITICAL TO YOUR SUCCESS

WE ALL KNOW who our external customers are. They're the customers who buy your product and pay your bills with the profits derived from the sale of goods. Your internal customers, however, are equally as important. The internal customers are those who support your efforts, are part of your high performing, successful team but do not buy products from you.

Anyone inside your organization who touches any process impacting a sale is an internal customer. These teammates could be shippers, receivers, janitors, warehouse staff, order pickers, those working at a sales and service counter, inside sales, or order desks, sales assistants, executive assistants, marketing teams, receptionists, inventory analysts, credit analysts, product specialists, I.T. support, project managers, quality assurance staff, safety teams, quotation personnel, sales managers, branch managers, a general manager or regional/district manager, a Vice President, CEO, CFP, or President. Regardless of the sector you work in as a professional seller, there are a myriad of people and processes that impact your ability to succeed. Each internal customer can open doors or create barriers to your success. You can safely assume, however, that not one sale will occur without an internal customer touching the process. I maintain that if the company who employs you, sells something then YOU are in sales.

From time to time there will be processes that don't go as planned, thwarting your sale. There will be times a department makes an error, resulting in a nastygram or phone call from a customer who received green apples when he ordered red apples. Resolving these issues quickly is how you will retain customers.

Picture yourself as a Sales Professional on the cusp of a major sale. The receptionist at your company has a crusty conversation with your buyer or depicts a poor image of the company, causing your purchaser to stop the buying process. One might think that would never happen, but it could. When I was a branch manager I had the best receptionist on earth. Marie Dowson would show up each and every day with the biggest smile and an energetic greeting for each staff member. Her voice smiled widely too. She was primed to make each person she contacted that day feel needed, respected, and valued. She recognized each of us as her internal customers and we valued her contribution to our team's success. The external customers adored her as well.

As a Sales Professional, the way you treat your internal customers will likely impact how they treat your external customers. Happy employees work harder and concentrate on the task at hand. They don't pick orders incorrectly, then say "Oh well I am just human" when they make a mistake. There will be a fine line between repeatedly accepting poor performance and understanding with empathy that mistakes can occur. Even you as the seller will mess up an order one day, perhaps inputting data incorrectly, resulting in that custom made product arriving without a key option.

Imagine you have waited 8 weeks for the factory ordered automobile to arrive. The day is drawing near and your external customer is calling you everyday, excited to see that beautiful gunmetal blue vehicle with the tan leather seats. Upon arrival, you discover the order entry person erred and ordered a black vehicle by mistake. Your external customer is now extremely disappointed, demands his deposit back, and walks away. How you react to your internal customer will impact not only on this lost sale, but potentially on your entire relationship going forward. The internal customer is likely not under your management responsibility, so their manager will or should be the one to address the situation. Your professional response needs to be one of understanding. Though you'll obviously be disappointed, ensure you don't burn the relational bridge. The person who erred will be totally embarrassed and feeling just as badly as you do.

More often that not your internal customers will perform in positive ways that assist you in reaching your goals and targets. ***It is imperative that you catch people doing things right and tell them so.*** Thank them for getting that order shipped or impacting on an important sale. Send them a thank you email and copy their boss. I once had a manager who preferred a particular brand of beverage. Because he was at times responsible for me being credited with a sale, I would occasionally drop off a case of his favorite beverage in his office. Thanking people in a tangible way is meaningful to them and shows them you appreciate the efforts being made in effort to see the team succeed. Remember that ***sales is a team sport***. Highly successful teams consist of internal customers built on trust. Steven Covey, author of the book, The 7 Habits of Highly Effective People once said, "Without trust we don't collaborate, we merely coordinate, and at best, cooperate. It is trust that transforms a group of people into a team."

As a Type A (Choleric) temperament, I recall times when I didn't interact effectively with internal customers as well as I should have.

My temperament, at times, impacted on my intensity, tenacity, and determination, resulting in bruised relationships. I recall a time that my internal customer, the credit manager, refused to approve a sale to one of my growing customers. A cold call had resulted in a new relationship that saw this customer convert nearly all his business to our company. The sales growth was exciting but as my customer's sales volume grew, his days to pay started to stretch, resulting in the credit manager's decision to push the pause button on approving more sales. I pressed him to open the account, and eventually wore him down. Several months later the customer filed for bankruptcy. Following the bankruptcy hearing in court, I took my credit manager to lunch and apologized for the part I played in the tragic outcome. In future years there were times when I may have disagreed with my credit manager but tried to see through the lens of his glasses more clearly. You and your credit manager are on the same team. As a Sales Professional it is natural to want every potential sale, especially if you have months of work invested. You must remember, though, that the sale isn't complete until the cheque clears the bank.

If, by chance, you are eventually promoted from professional seller to a sales manager, ensure your internal customers are placed in positions that provide them the greatest chance for growth and success. I maintain that had Wayne Gretzky played goal, he would have failed. Instead, he was placed in a different position as a young kid and is now arguably, considered the best hockey player in NHL history. Content employees, playing the right positions, treated with respect, and remunerated fairly, are loyal employees and effective internal customers.

As often as possible, ensure your relationships with all your internal customers stay intact. The respect you'll garner from them will impact your success trajectory in a dramatic fashion.

17

VALUE ADDED SELLING

THE VOICE OF Experience interviews you've read have some common denominators. In each case the sales professionals, regardless of the number of years in their respective fields, each identified a trait or skill set that impacted on their success. Not one of them said "I am a great closer or a great negotiator." The words we saw were integrity, empathy, honesty, grit, perseverance, effective probing skills, self motivation, friendliness, and consideration.

Your sales manager will talk about consultative selling and adding value. At the front end of your career, you will nod and smile, all the time wondering what he or she is talking about. Always ask for clarity when something is stated that you can easily see is important to the speaker and equally important to the selling process, yet might be a new word in your new world.

Perhaps your coach or sales manager starts talking about value added selling. Consider that you are a consumer. What do you value when making a buying decision? If you are walking around the auto dealership what is your attention drawn to first? My gut says you look at that price tag hanging from the rearview mirror or maybe the entire side of the truck says "$11,000 off." We often see the phrase "Employee pricing until month end—you pay what we pay." Yes, we all need to consider the price of large purchases.

For every product or service you sell or provide there will be a price and value. They are not the same. The price is simple. What you get for the price paid is the perceived value. Once you purchase the product you realize whether you received the expected value or not. If not, you experience buyer's remorse and potentially have 30 days to return the product. If you just bought a house and didn't want to hire a house inspector prior to the removal of conditions, later you might discover that the roof leaks, or the furnace or hot water tank is failing. You cannot return that purchase. The value added realtor will urge you to get a house inspection.

While a product has a price and value, you as the professional seller add value too. You bring product or industry expertise. Your product knowledge is substantial. It is knowledge not every other seller has. You have insight into your product that the customer would not otherwise have any way to discover other than through you. Your role is to be recognized as a 'solutions guru.' You will often be the conduit between the manufacturer of the product and the eventual user, your customer. ***When presenting your product, do not start with the price.*** Professional Sales people begin with determining needs, then presenting the matching features, benefits, and value, followed by the price when asked.

Differentiate yourself and you'll add value to your customer's buying process. Don't just be another seller. Don't be afraid of being different, but be better than all the other sellers that the customer has come into contact with. Utilize the sales process. Ask appropriate and nonthreatening questions, look your customer in the eye and show that you care about their stated needs. Develop a habit of being a collaborative seller. This is where you AND your customer work together to develop an endorsed solution. When your customer contributes to the solution, they will be quicker to endorse your recommendation, and buy what you're selling. When you and your customer are on the same page, working on a common goal, it reduces the possibility they seek a competitor's solutions. Effective questioning allows for their input. Take away their problem, then follow it through to satisfaction.

Perhaps your realtor reveals that just behind the property you want to purchase, a 24 hour gas station was just approved by city council. Do you still want to proceed to buy the property? The realtor added value by being open and honest regarding the gas station. Perhaps the car dealer tells you the car you have interest in appears to have been in a previous accident. He likely ran a Carfax search and added value through showing his or her level of integrity.

You could be selling a product you know will be discontinued soon because your company has asked you to clear out the old stock. Ensure you share that information. I have found that a customer often purchases a product today, then wants five more a year later to match what he bought initially. This is your integrity and honesty on the line. Yes products can cease to be manufactured without notice, but successful Sales Professionals add value by staying engaged in the process from presentation, through the sale, to following up after the customer has installed or used the product, ensuring 100% satisfaction of the product. When the customer buys again, chances are they will buy from you. Do not become a hit and run specialist, who sells a substandard product and is afraid to follow up, knowing there may already be a quality concern.

You become your customer's trusted advisor and consultant by adding value. Develop great practises and habits at the front end of your career so you don't need to make challenging process changes later.

Repeat with me: "I commit myself to be a value-added Sales Professional."

BALKTALK #14 – Negotiating a Win-Win

In the process of buying and selling, each person wants to feel as though they won the better side of the equation. A few years ago I planned to purchase a Mercedes Smart Car for my wife. Following my thorough online research I found exactly what we wanted, but the dealership was two hours from my house. Additionally the vehicle seemed exceedingly overpriced. I thought that an ad error may have occurred. I spoke to the sales person by phone and queried him on whether the price was accurate. He confirmed it was. I then revealed my research indicated it appeared drastically overpriced in comparison to other Smart cars in comparable years and options. After a few minutes I stated that "I am buying a Smart car today and will make you an offer now. If you accept it, I will bring you a certified cheque tomorrow and buy it, providing the car is as advertised." I then offered him 40% less than the vehicle was listed at. He stated that his sales manager was on vacation that day and he could not authorize such a low price, but stated he would try to track down his manager. Within a half hour he called and accepted the offer. The following day I drove the two hours, inspected the vehicle and completed the purchase. When I asked why the car had been priced so high and why he accepted my offer he revealed the car had been on their sales lot for one year. The previous used car manager had purchased it at the auction and overpaid for it, then became determined not to sell it below cost. He was absolutely thrilled to finally get rid of the car, since the sales staff had been staring at it for a year. I was thrilled because I found the exact vehicle I wanted at the right price with the exact options, low mileage, and in the exact colour preferred. It even still smelled new.

This was a win-win. Both parties walked away happy. The other win-win was due to the purchase occurring on the last day of the month, the car dealership was potentially more motivated to sell in effort to hit their sales budget for the month and I was fortunate to get the vehicle at the reduced price = win-win.

There will be tough negotiations in your selling journey. They might not all be price-oriented, but many will be. When either party is determined to see the other party lose, it will not result in a win-win. As a Sales Professional it is your goal to be flexible enough, yet confident enough in your solution to convince your customer that he or she is getting great value at the price point stated. Often both parties will have to provide some flexibility in their stance to see the win-win occur. By showing some flexibility this time, the boomerang effect will benefit you next time.

Showing your customer that you truly desire a win-win is certain to strengthen your relationship, build the bridge of trust, and see him return to you for his future needs.

18

MANAGING YOUR OPPORTUNITY FUNNEL

YOU WON'T BE far into your new career when you will start to experience a bit of anxiety as to how to manage all the opportunities (opps) that have landed in your funnel. Opportunities are not created equal. Every conversation you have with a client or prospective customer might uncover an opportunity that then gets dropped into your funnel. If not well managed, your funnel will fill to capacity and those that overflow or evaporate might well have become a sale. Once it is out of view and possibly out of mind, you are unlikely to ever take action on it.

Opportunities are categorized by temperature. I would draw a huge funnel on an 8 ½" x 11" white page and write my opportunities as they occurred. You might elect to use a large sheet of bristle board or another visual tool. Depending on your sales sector, you will have short cycle opps and long cycle opps. Industrial selling can see short cycle opps potentially mature into a sale immediately, even prior to plotting them. As you find yourself getting busier you'll discover you simply cannot plot them all. Apply a minimum dollar value to the opps that will be plotted into your funnel.

If you are in real estate, basically every home you show, every client you meet and each open house you hold will uncover new contacts and opportunities for which to provide a solution. Recall one of my guests, Mark Morris, who is the classic 'don't give up' guy. He follows up every single opportunity until it is lost and still wants to know why it resulted in a loss. He manages his funnel extremely well.

Managing your funnel requires daily review. This is when you plot the opps inside the funnel. The hot opps are nearest the bottom funnel opening because that is where the $ sign is. When it drops out of the funnel it is a sale. The warm opps are within the next level. These could be either opps that are medium cycle opps or those you actually expect to mature into sales but will take a bit more work to satisfy the buyer. Perhaps he has already stated that he will be ready in May for the new car or his building will be finished in February and a security system will be needed. It is imperative you don't lose sight of the warm opps.

The lukewarm opps are the next level and could easily graduate to warm, given the right timing and circumstances but likewise could change to cold or evaporate out through the top of the open funnel. It is important that you stay in contact with those you sense are lukewarm. Circumstances change quickly and if you suddenly disappear, lose contact or appear disinterested, you can easily be forgotten. You might discover later that the sale did occur but another company enjoyed the purchase order.

Cold opportunities aren't necessarily cold from the start. By asking appropriate open-ended questions you may want to plot them lower in the funnel. If an opportunity has been floating for an extended period, you have the option of removing it, or you might give it another week or month to mature. That is your call. There is no hard and fast rule on how long to allow one temperature to exist before taking action. If the sale is lost for any reason, it is simply removed.

It is also important to have a good idea as to when the opp will mature. This allows you to assess what the next quarter of your year is looking like. You might not quite be at 25% of budget after Q1 but you know your hot opps are going to gush out the bottom of the funnel in Q2 or your lukewarm opp has been promised to you in Q3. This is why it is so critical to manage the funnel process with accuracy and be positioned to make quality assessments when your manager calls.

Just before I retired we landed a large order that I had pursued for four months and twice was told there would be no sale. I had left it in the cold section of my funnel and drove past the jobsite every Monday. One day at lunch hour I saw a truck on the job site so I just dropped in and was able to engage the business owner in a deeper conversation. Up until this point we had only chatted by phone, but had never met. Each time we did speak, he had said he had no need for my services. I persevered, however, and after this meeting in person, the cold opp graduated to a hot one in only three weeks. In this case he was about to make a substantial online purchase for new LED lighting fixtures for his new welding factory. Online buying meant he might potentially have a challenge with warranty issues, could not physically see a sample fixture pre-purchase, wasn't certain of its quality, would have no local support if any challenges occurred with shipping damage, and had not seen an actual engineered, professionally designed lighting solution. He was preparing to purchase what he thought he needed. In essence, I quickly became his trusted advisor based on my knowledge and access to an engineered solution. Once I was able to show him an actual product, provide a better warranty than he was considering, and gained his confidence, he moved ahead with the purchase. Had I been content to leave the opportunity in the cold section or allowed it to evaporate, a sale would never have culminated.

You might hear someone say to grab the low hanging fruit. Imagine an apple orchard and each apple is a sales opportunity. The fruit at the bottom is easy to pick, requires little effort and can fill a basket (funnel) without much effort. The quality of the low hanging fruit is not nearly as tasty as the fruit at the top of the tree that has had added exposure to the sun and rain. That fruit ripens faster. The low hanging fruit has been in the shade much of the time, has seen less sun and rain and is thus potentially smaller and less delectable. The analogy is clear. It is well worth your effort to get to the top of the tree, and pick the ripest fruit (opportunities). Your reward will be far tastier, more profitable sales. The more effort you put into succeeding, the more satisfying it is to celebrate a victory. Allow your competitors to eat the sour apples.

Obviously, added attention will be drawn to hot opps or those you can see graduating quickly from warm to hot. I had a sales manager who used the term 'closest to cash' and encouraged us to invest our time there first. This made sense to me. We all like to be close to cash.

Balance your time, while managing your funnel effectively so you don't get trapped in the 'paralysis of anaylsis.' Certain temperaments can be more prone to this than others. You need to quickly make your temperature assessments, create an action plan for each opportunity, set some time guidelines for each, and take action.

I love the funnel management process. Draw your funnel, get a highlighter and begin. Get closer to cash!

VOICE OF EXPERIENCE — Janelle Balkwill B.A.,
M.Cl Sc. RAUD, RHIP, Aud (C) — Clinical Audiologist

Q – What age were you when you began your professional sales career?

A – 24.

Q – What were you selling at that point in your career?

A – Hearing aids and all related audiological services.

Q – How many years have you been a full time professional sales person?

A – I have been selling for 6 years but consider myself more of a medical professional than a true sales person. I did, however, quickly learn that a key part of my success journey as a Clinical Audiologist would include selling.

Q – Looking back, how well prepared were you for the selling aspect of your career on day one?

A – Extremely underprepared. I had absolutely no formal sales training.

Q – Talk about year one as a professional sales representative.

A – It was almost a fake it til ya make it mentality really, but then through experience, some success and failure, and mentoring, I became more comfortable with the fact that I was now in a position where my advice was literally changing people's lives. I found this to be very gratifying.

Q – Has discouragement ever been a challenge at any point? If so, how did you journey through it initially?

A – Yes for sure. Initially I felt like I wasn't very good at my job if I failed to hit the sales targets for the month. The worst aspect of that was I didn't know what to change or what strategies I could adopt to improve the sales performance. I really didn't want to sell so I wasn't that eager to learn how to improve. I wanted to have an ethical practice that I could be proud of. I saw selling as a dirty word that would contradict what I had learned along the path to becoming an Audiologist. I soon learned that I can do both, by providing sound, ethical advice, and at the same time, retain my own integrity in the process.

Q – What was/is the biggest challenge you face on a regular basis in sales?

A – To me, it is important that my patients don't feel like they are sold a product they don't need. I don't want to be seen as that high pressure seller. I accurately perform the hearing tests required to make a professional assessment then provide the options that will enhance their relationships and quality of life. I recognize we still have monthly targets for sales but I feel confident that if I perform my duties well, the sales will come, and so far that is exactly what has occurred.

Q – What has been the most substantial factor to any success you have experienced?

A – It seems that my patients really like me and trust my assessments. They don't hesitate to take my advice. When they accept they have a hearing deficiency, and want a solution, it is my responsibility to provide a solution within their budgetary constraints. I get a lot of joy and satisfaction by having strong relationships with my patients too.

Q – Has there been one key person who has consistently impacted on your success journey? Would you consider that person to be your mentor?

A – Yes, my Dad. He has been instrumental in showing me that selling is not a dirty word but is simply the provision of a solution to somebody's problem. He has shared many of his own failures in his own sales roles too which helps me. He is quick to encourage me in my journey as well.

Q – When you experience a successful chapter in your journey do you allow yourself to bask in the sunshine?

A – Yes, for a moment, but then it is time to get working on the next goal. I tend to always be looking ahead vs back.

Q – How many hours a week do you work on average?

A – 38-40 since I am in a clinical environment with normal hours.

Q – What one skill set has had the most significant impact on your success to date?

A – Probably my personality. I am a positive, friendly, energetic person. I think I have a good likeability factor, along with a high degree of empathy, sincerity, reliability, and integrity. I seem to receive high praise from my patients who have been gracious in giving me many referrals too, which is essential in my business. I know I am adding value to my patients' lives, so being able to provide a tangible benefit to them is extremely satisfying to me.

Q – What would you regard as your most significant professional regret to date?

A – At this point I can honestly say I have no regrets. The decisions I have made so far have proven beneficial so I guess I will keep doing what I am doing, while seeking continual ways to improve.

Q – Talk briefly on any challenge(s) regarding work/life balance and how you navigate that?

A – I am fortunate to have a Monday to Friday role with regular office hours. I work by appointment only therefore I know that at the end of the day I can leave work and enjoy my home and social life.

Q – How has the COVID-19 pandemic impacted on your role?

A – Our company closed all the clinical offices for a period and I was selected to look after 12 clinics across British Columbia. All email, phone calls, and customer needs were funnelled to me. I wasn't seeing patients face to face for a while since our doors were closed and locked. I did experience some level of stress that felt a bit foreign to me, simply due to the workload and expectations of customers all across the province. Once the office reopened I had to adjust to new protocols and scheduling all the patients who were eager to be seen. Things are somewhat back to normal now and sales have been buoyant.

Q – What key piece of advice would you offer to the person who is just beginning their career as a Sales Professional?

A – I would strongly suggest they get formally trained in selling. I still consider myself relatively new in selling and am learning day by day. My sales skills are developing but can see now that some sales training at the front end would have been extremely beneficial.

Q – What would the experienced Janelle tell the young Janelle on day one of her career?

A – Accept that though your career is one of a professional Clinical Audiologist, you also will be selling hearing aids and associated services. Get comfortable asking the right questions about customer budgets, develop the skill of handling objections, and always ask for the order. If the customer hesitates, gently probe as to why there is hesitation. This has been a challenge but I think I am improving.

BALKTALK #15 – There is a Substantial Cost to Employ You

Regardless of the product or service you sell, there is a cost to your employer to have you on the team. Your responsibility is to pay for yourself and after having done so, ensure your employer has profit dollars left in their coffers. Over the course of your career, especially after your selling skills have become well developed, you might find other companies sending headhunters to determine your level of loyalty or contentment with your current employer. My suggestion is to be grateful toward your employer. They are the one with all the risk. They gave you a chance to become a Sales Professional. Jumping jobs every two years sends a dangerous message to an employer reviewing your LinkedIn profile.

Here are some potential costs to employing you: salary, commission or bonus, health benefits, RSP or 401K company contributions, desk rental fee, advertising costs, business cards, vacation pay, sick days taken, automobile provision or associated coverages for mileage paid, automobile lease paid or fuel and maintenance, employee assistance plan, laptop, cell phone allowance, company apparel, flights, hotels, personal meals, expense accounts, social outings with customers, training and on-boarding, ongoing training, seminars, and professional or industry membership fees. These are hard costs to your employer. Soft costs are complacency, theft, and sick time taken without cause. Complacency and discouragement robs your employer of productivity and profit. Be aware of all these costs and consider each one when a new opportunity comes knocking, because it will.

Your reputation as a high achieving Sales Professional will be noticed within your business sector and your services will be desired. There are a myriad of other considerations to be undertaken before jumping ship of course. Get out a sheet of paper and make your pros and cons list.

19

NEVER GIVE UP

IF YOU CAME into your career confidently convinced you have a sincere, burning passion for selling, you will never feel like giving up. *I am just kidding of course.* There will be days or chapters in your professional journey where those dreaded voices will be whispering statements that if adopted, will derail your journey. Babe Ruth said **"It's hard to beat a person who never gives up."**

I recently attended a trade show where the luncheon keynote speaker was Ryan Walter, who played for the Montreal Canadiens in 1993, winning the Stanley Cup. While he was speaking, he removed his Stanley Cup ring and passed it around the room of 300. I was the last person to see it and hold it. I returned it to him and had a nice chat. I now have a photo of me wearing a Stanley Cup ring. How cool is that?

Ryan spoke of the strength and resilience of that team and how hard it is to win a Cup. He replayed the 10 overtime games they won to achieve that goal. He recalled every single player who had gone beyond the call so they could win as a team. That team had some Hall of Famers but also some who were grinder type players. Each played a critical role in winning the Cup. It is a gruelling regular season schedule, then 16 or more playoff games at yet another level of intensity and commitment. Many players have injuries, bruises, and pulled muscles. We've heard of players playing with broken ribs or a separated shoulder. *He really zeroed in on one word—resilience.*

When I think of someone close to me who has shown resilience I think of my eldest daughter, Katelyn. She and her sister had set a goal to each become speech pathologists and work together in their own clinic. Our younger daughter Janelle then asked to volunteer at a speech therapy clinic and discovered she wouldn't enjoy speech pathology as a career. Her school counsellor stated that all her university courses would benefit her in audiology, if that were of interest. Janelle agreed.

Katelyn still pursued Speech Pathology, but with only 33 new student spots available and over 400 applicants, she wasn't accepted at the graduate university she applied to. She then took another year of university to upgrade and reapplied. This time her professor stated she would most likely be accepted, considering she held an 88% average, yet again was not. Showing extreme resilience, though discouraged, she changed lanes, returned to university, and pursued a Bachelor of Education. She is now a teacher. Being an accomplished pianist she teaches music, drama and science. Along the journey there was extreme disappointment and temptation to give up. She didn't and has been rewarded.

The word 'resilience' resonates with me because it is most definitely a required element to succeeding in professional selling. It will be one of your greatest attributes, along with all the other traits I have introduced to you thus far. You will have times when the sales seem to come easily and there will be dry times when you might experience an emotional basement chapter. This happened to me in my life insurance career and the voices I heard and adopted, eliminated me from succeeding at that time. Over the years I have become extremely resilient and have overcome many bumps and bruises; physically, financially, emotionally, and spiritually. In my selling career I was often defined as tenacious. I simply refused to give up. My journey and story continues.

Speaking of giving up, in July 2020 my daughter, Katelyn and I were driving on what would have been a ten hour journey. We were only 3 hours from our starting point when all the traffic stopped. The trucker in front of us advised we would be 2 hours getting through. Two sections of road had been washed away by flooding. One lane of alternating traffic was being allowed to pass through, literally while they completed the road repair. He said we were 35 km from the area that had been washed out.

Well, two hours passed, then three, then four. Now there were times when no cars were going in either direction for 20 minutes at a time and people were out walking, jogging, removing their bicycles, and riding up to see what was going on. Then we were told we would be six hours getting through. Many drivers gave up, turned and went back from whence they came. After five hours and 55 minutes the trucker jumped out of his big rig and ran back to us and pointed at a road sign which said 2 km to a certain small town which was where the washout was. Eventually there was a 1 km sign. Katelyn and I were high fiving one another. We now could see the heavy equipment, backhoes, trucks and huge vacuums being used to remove water. We were 5 minutes to victory when I looked in my rear view mirror and about 10 or 15 cars behind us, I saw a car pull out and go the other way. They had sat for nearly 6 hours and were 10 minutes from their goal when they gave up. They weren't at the point where they could see the equipment we saw. They didn't know how close they were to victory.

As a professional seller, you never know when you'll be five minutes from victory. One more sales call, one more phone call, one more attempt to close that sale. Perhaps you have one more month to hit a sales budget or one more year to be profitable. Len Filiault, one of my guests, said his wife gave him five years to become successful in the real estate business. Yet due to his extreme resilience, getting a mentor and his determination to succeed, he was ahead of schedule by 3 years.

Adopt resiliency, get a mentor and adopt a 'never give up' attitude. It worked for Len and it will work for you too.

I encourage you to never accept, adopt, or say out loud that you have failed. Do not allow those words to take root in your brain. Dolly Parton stated "I don't feel like a failure just because something I tried failed." Can you imagine the setbacks and levels of challenge she experienced during her dream, creation, and building of Dollywood? If ever in Pigeon Forge, Tennessee be sure to visit her magnificent theme park.

Failure is simply a process or action you took that didn't succeed. You now know what doesn't work. Try something else, or another method. Actual failing occurs when you quit and give up and refuse to try again. I gave up on selling life insurance but I didn't give up my passion for selling.

Many millionaires and billionaires have experienced bankruptcy but didn't give up. Walt Disney, P.T. Barnum, George Foreman, and Elton John are amongst those who didn't give up. You will be rewarded too, by refusing to give up. Giving up after the knock down is too easy. Getting up after the knock down is where your growth and show of courage occurs.

I can sense your passion for selling and know you are the kind of person that won't quit. The bridge to success is just down the road 5 minutes. There's no turning back now!

20

CONCLUSION

Four Decades of Selling Success

WHEN I REALIZE I actually invested four decades of my life in the selling sector, I reminisce about the life lessons I have benefitted from. I asked each of my Voice of Experience guests what the experienced salesperson of today would tell the new inexperienced salesperson on day one of their individual career. I asked myself the same question. Here are my thoughts:

- Be certain you have a passion for selling
- Develop your core values and live by them
- List your life priorities and refer to them when challenging decisions need to be made
- Recognize that relationships will be far more important than any financial victory
- Realize you cannot do it alone. Surround yourself with smart people who work hard
- Catch people doing things right and tell them so

- Don't fear change. Accept it and embrace it
- Take calculated risks
- Develop your emotional balance. Don't get too high or too low
- Celebrate successes as they occur
- Don't get stuck at a job or company you cannot thrive in
- Find a mentor at the front end of your career
- Prepare and be open to becoming a mentor
- Ask forgiveness *when* you mess up—not *if* you mess up
- Grant forgiveness when asked for it. Rinse the slate and move on
- Don't ever lose your sense of humor. You'll need it to survive the journey
- Adopt a continuous improvement motto for yourself. Never stop learning
- Laugh everyday and have fun at work
- Don't let business losses dictate your sense of happiness
- Adopt the Golden Rule (treat others as you want to be treated)

Please marinate these words: ***You don't immediately have to be great at everything or perfect at every single aspect of the sales process to succeed. Just keep improving.***

I have made many mistakes and failed often over four decades. I have shared many embarrassing blunders with you. My goal herein was to share what I know works and what I realize failed. I want you to know that I experienced fear, intimidation, unqualified thoughts, heard all those voices, lost focus, failed often and felt totally discouraged and defeated at times. I have experienced disappointment or anger at certain situations, and some of it pointed at myself. I don't trust easily nor immediately, and can be cynical at times. I regret that I negatively impacted some valuable relationships over 40 years as well. I do however maintain that the rear view mirror is very small for a reason. The windshield is what we're supposed to be focused on, looking ahead, anticipating a great future.

Looking to the past can provide certain benefits but there is no point in wallowing in past failures and defeat. Learn and move forward!

This book is not about my raging success, but is about *your* raging success. I cannot relive the last four decades but you can live the next four decades. Commit to live with the least amount of regret you can. Set your core values and commit to live by them. Get a mentor and be a mentor. A person with one year's experience has 365 more days than the person starting his or her selling career on day one. Reach out and offer a hand. Don't wait four decades to share your knowledge and insights.

To close, allow me to thank you for investing your personal time in reading my book. I sincerely believe it will send you on an incredible trajectory, elevating your selling skills during your professional selling journey. *You will graduate from a sales person to a Sales Professional!*

As you develop a love and passion for selling, my hope for you is incredible success!

Good Selling.

Sincerely,
Greg

FINAL THOUGHTS AND THANKS

Writing this book has been a journey through most of my life in general, with focus on my selling experiences. Reliving it has evoked many emotions. Specifically it caused me to reflect on who my mentors were and how they each impacted on my life in general; not only my life in the selling arena. I want to pay tribute to a few of them here.

Parents – (posthumously) few people succeed in life without guidance, direction and assistance throughout each chapter of their upbringing. Dad taught me that I had to develop strong work habits and how to be productive each day. Mom lovingly caught me doing things right and encouraged me in anything and everything I tried.

Orion Snyder – (posthumously) the gentleman who owned the men's clothing store in Harrow. He gave me my first opportunity to watch 'someone on stage' and learn how to sell.

Allan Parr – as a young teenager, Al provided me employment at his horse ranch and later in his electrical contracting business. He was like a second dad to me.

Bernard Calhoun – (posthumously)—a man with a great attitude. I spent countless hours and weekends showing horses with him and his wife and they always welcomed me in their home.

Larry Mills – a quiet high quality man of resilience who successfully overcame obstacles in his journey. As a young adult I was watching carefully. He and his wife Sharon always had a pot of coffee ready.

Mark Hazzard – my Pastor for 25 years but more importantly a great friend and confidant.

Jim Lawton – he and his wife Donna were instrumental in quietly guiding Elli and I in developing our parenting style. Jim has walked with me through the last 43 years of my life, providing valuable counsel and friendship.

ACKNOWLEDGEMENTS

The 6 Voice of Experience guests. Thanks for your time, your honesty, transparency and willingness to contribute to my book.

Nicole Lamont – my Editor, who allowed me to capitalize the phrase 'Sales Professional' throughout my book, and was so flexible and easy to work with.

Sloane Kini – my SPS Coach—thank you for all your direction, guidance, and support at each phase of the writing and publishing process.

Family – One cannot walk this journey without love, patience and support. My sisters, Bonny (Carl) and Lori (Dan) and my immediate family, Elli, Katelyn and Janelle have been consistently encouraging throughout the travels and experiences of my life and during the process of writing this book. I love and appreciate you all.

Made in the USA
Monee, IL
20 August 2021